# GRICIN

8 P

## 35023

# THE REAL STORY OF THE RAILWAY CHILDREN

# Introduction

In the words of Dylan Thomas, 'Begin at the beginning'; a Saturday morning, in 1954, and being taken, by my Dad, to see a train crash in Leeds New City Station. An engine had mounted the buffers and come to rest at the ticket barrier, being witness to this crash was, for me, the beginning of a lifetime connection with the railway, and the steam locomotives which powered it. 'Gricing' could be considered a crash course in my sixty years of involvement with the railway, in almost every aspect of its being.

My career, with British Railways, was as an engine cleaner and fireman, firstly at Farnley Junction, (55C), followed by spells at Stewarts Lane, (73A) very briefly, at Nine Elms (70A), where I had 3 glorious years, several months working out of Holbeck, (55A), and a final year and a half at Belle Vue, Wakefield, (56A), from where I was made redundant. These seven years at 'the coal face' included such joys as cleaning mangled pieces of cow from various low-hanging parts of Jubliee Class 4-6-0 No.45695 Minotaur, she'd ploughed into a herd of them, at speed. Engine cleaning, there was much more to it than shiney paintwork! The mangled cows were a salutary introduction to life as an engine cleaner, at the tender age of 15; however, gruesome as this incident was, it didn't deter me from my involvement in matters railway, not even redundancy stopped that.

Over the 40 odd years since steam traction ceased to be the driving force on the National Railway network, and I became 'surplus to their requirements', I've scribbled a few railway related articles, in enthusiast magazines and newspapers, written three books, and taken a few photographs, some of which have been published. In the days before the 'Internet', from 1989 to 1993, I wiled away the time by self-publishing and distributing the only national heritage railway timetable - 'Wilson's Preserved Steam Railway Timetable'. Some of my other railway entanglements have been; as a volunteer, with the Association of Railway Preservation Societies, (now the Heritage Railway Association), staging a Red Nose event, with the help of Andrew Naish and the Great Central Railway, a win, win, thing in which money was raised for Comic Relief by taking a trainload of children with disabilities, and their carers, for a day out on the railway, the more able-bodied kids got the chance to 'cab' No. 35005 Canadian Pacific. Currently I'm a member of the 82045 Locomotive Trust helping to raise money for and awareness of this excellent scheme.

On the academic front I spent several years researching; railway labour, the railway races to the North, and heritage railways, in the reading room at the National Railway Museum, (NRM). Prior to my labours in the reading room I had 3 years at the University of Leeds gaining a BA in Philosophy and the History of Science, learning, in the process, how to interpret and write about historical subjects. Following my researches, and my graduation, I was invited to speak at International Conferences, on Railway related topics, at the NRM. However, I consider my most important contribution to all things railway was to have been behind Joe Duddington and Tommy Bray being recognised and celebrated for their achievement in setting the world speed record for a steam locomotive. My campaign, which lasted almost two years, culminated in a leading article in the Guardian's Society section, in May 2002. "Mallard became a legend when it smashed the speed record for a steam locomotive. But who remembers the crew? With lottery money now helping to chronicle the golden age of trains, one man is refusing to accept the way workers have been airbrushed from Britain's railway history." (Front page, Society Guardian, The Guardian, May 1st 2002).

It had the desired effect. Duddington and Bray's names were put in the cab of No. 60022 / 4468 Mallard, they were also included in the museum's Visitor's guide book, and on the information panels placed around the locomotive, as well as having their story told to visitors of the museum by 'explainers'.

'Gricing' however, is more than the body of research, my 7 years as a professional footplateman, and years of active involvement, at different levels, within railway preservation; 'Gricing' is a view of the railway as; a catalyst and a sewer, from God's wonderful to God's dead, contradictions and connections both real and imagined, from all our yesterdays to all of our if only's, could have's, might have been's.

There are a few other things I would ask the reader to keep in mind as you travel with me through my railway mindscape. In writing 'Gricing' I was making a deliberate and conscious attempt to write about the railway and railway preservation in a manner which went beyond liveries, dates and counting rivets. Writing about 'historical' events you inevitably have one foot in the past, if only as something to push against, to move forward from what has gone before. I had in mind a desire to give the reader an insight into the way my own experiences, my own unique path across the railway landscape, shaped and formed the opinions I have put forward in the book. Remember all this as you read 'Gricing' because 'Gricing' isn't a rose tinted view, or a benign retrospective. There are, undoubtedly, aspects of Gricing which, to some of you, will seem quite critical; I make no apologies for this. 'Gricing' wasn't written with a view to gaining universal approval, rather it was written to express my own point of view on a subject, an industry, and a hobby, which has been an essential part of my life for 6 decades.

All the photographs are my own and the work has been proof-read by my friend, partner, and wife Dr. Anne Marie Wilson.

It is dedicated to my parents Arnold and Marjorie Wilson and to railwaymen everywhere.

# All Aboard

Roll up, roll up, and buy a platform ticket, back, back to the days when the world was driven by steam. No need for a passport, baggage check, or sleeping in an airport lounge, just turn up and fill your lungs with the devil's own brew of hot oil and sulphur  and you're there.

Sinews have been strained, in an almost heroic effort, to seek out the most 'rose tinted' of steam railway spectacles; Chocolate and Cream, Blood and Custard, Brunswick Green and BR Black, Garter Blue and Crimson Lake, cycling lions - coats of arms, and country stations. Trains, you want them, we've got them, mixed goods or minerals, the TPO and Auto train, mainline expresses and branch line locals. Signals; ground, fixed, or semaphore, tunnels, bridges and viaducts - no line has been left un-ballasted.

Ex-GWR Hall Class 4-6-0, No.4936 Kinlet Hall, crossing Oldbury viaduct – Severn Valley Railway.

Back in those days which were, naturally, halcyon the monthly 'must read' for a good many teenage boys was O.S. Nock's column in Railway Magazine, 'Locomotive Practice and Performance'.  As the years, too many for my liking, have gone by I learned that the word 'performance' had several, sometimes conflicting, interpretations. 'Gricing', is about performance in its theatrical sense - every photograph is a stage set with a scene and actors, some human, others industrial machinery. Taking part in railway preservation and operation is to star in a reality re-creation of an imagined reality – a sort of reality plus. In these photographs the object of the camera is to tell the most believable lie - the nearer falsity represents the 'imagined' reality the better the picture - in the quasi-

Orwellian world of Heritage where reality is, quite simply, made up. In fact re-writing history, often the same bits over and over again, is a major contributor to the genre of 'railway literature'. Unfortunately, for the most part, they completely miss the point, giving priority to dates, liveries, and names at the expense of explanation, context and change.

Ex-BR Class 4 4-6-0, No.75029, at Beck Hole, with a goods working for Goathland on the NYMR.

The steam locomotives themselves are, undoubtedly, the stars of the 'Heritage Railway Show' but, without a supporting cast of coaches and signals, stations and bridges, and an ambience provided by, amongst other things, appropriately dressed volunteers there would be no show. Running a theatre which covers 5, 10, even 20 miles of the countryside with multiple stages, in carriages, or on platforms, not to mention signal boxes, sheds, and footplates, with a cast of thousands is a performance in itself. When you are doing all this; rebuilding the sets, training the actors, writing new scripts, and trying to satisfy a hypercritical audience, this is the triumph of optimism over adversity and is to be applauded. However, a note of caution, worthy and worthwhile as this endeavour is, it is as near to the reality of the revenue earning railway of the early to mid-20th century as Celebrity Big Brother is to George Orwell's dystopian vision of Post-war Britain – "1984".

 The very existence of Heritage Railways came about because a relatively small number of people, (some sources quote 36, I'll settle for about as many as you could get into the public room of a Birmingham city centre hotel circa 1950), persuaded tens of thousands of other people that they wanted to hang on to something, so badly, that they would undertake an enormous diversity of tasks; raising vast sums of money, we're talking in the tens if not hundreds of millions of pounds, rebuilding rusted hulks; in a water meadow, under tarpaulin, during a large part of the rebuilding of one former Southern Railway Pacific, (No. 35027 Port Line was partially re-built in a field at Blunsdon alongside the Swindon & Cricklade Railway), and if that wasn't daunting enough there was petitioning everyone from the local parish councillor and MP, to Parliament and the European Union. Simply mobilising and then providing a long term incentive for such a vast, socially, and geographically diverse volunteer workforce should not be under-estimated – without this volunteer army there would be no 'Heritage Railway'.

'Maroon' Ex-LMS Class 8F 2-8-0, No.48624, approaching Quorn & Woodhouse on the Great Central Railway.

Today, volunteering can be a way to get a job, but in 1950s Britain being a 'volunteer' as part of your leisure activity, was a very novel idea. The volunteer railwaymen, and women, weren't, in general, blue collar workers, far from it. The movement was led, by engineers, university students and lecturers, lawyers, and accountants, members of the professional classes. In the beginning, despite the blue collar nature of what was, supposedly, being preserved by the railway preservationists there was very little input from working railwaymen. Leaving aside the meagre level of input from rank and file railwaymen the vast army, of unsung volunteers, (in the very early days on the Talyllyn, some of the volunteers were actually men 'on loan' from the armed forces doing their 'National Service'), may not have moved heaven and earth but they did lay/relay miles of track, move entire stations, signal boxes, bridges, turntables, and even a cast iron Gents urinal, around the country in attempting to re-create 'authentic' backdrops, with correctly liveried motive power and rolling stock to maintain the illusion that 1950 something was alive and well. Should anyone doubt this just ask yourself – why, in six decades of railway preservation, no one has painted a GWR Castle class 4-6-0 yellow or turned out one of Stanier's 'workhorse' 8F 2-8-0s in Lilac with a matching pink tender sporting a coat of arms which looked suspiciously like a Barbie Doll riding My Little Pony. But then there is this livery, currently, being carried by 48624 and there's that South Yorkshireman Headboard – right line, but the wrong engine and the wrong livery!

No.2 at Andrews House Station - Tanfield Railway.

There have been one or two other excursions into 'own brand' liveries, most notably, perhaps, in the early days of the Keighley and Worth Valley Railway, but these have, mercifully, been relatively short-lived. Had someone been foolhardy enough to paint so venerated an artefact as one of God's Wonderful Railway's Castle Class locomotives yellow it is a safe bet that they too would have been relatively short-lived.

Another indicator of the importance of the 'overall ambience' is to be found on the platforms of the preserved stations themselves. Heritage Railway stations carry advertisements for such bygone products as; Brasso, Virol, because, apparently, 'anaemic girls need it' and Fry's Five Boys chocolate bars - on the station at Boat of Garten there's even a black and white enamel advertisement for 'McGrowther's Pork Sausages'- an off-spin of McGrowler's Pork pies no doubt. What these stations do not have are advertisements for Sony Playstation, Samsung Mobile phones and Sky TV.

Ex-SR BoB Class 4-6-2, No.34053 Sir Keith Park, at Haye Bridge, on the Severn Valley Railway.

Some lines boast of still having gas lighting on their stations, others that they have turned former goods sheds into cafes or small exhibits museums, sometimes both, but they don't have MacDonald's, Subway, or Starbucks outlets in place of the Refreshment Rooms. Modern life and the modern built environment are to be kept out at all costs - pies, real ale, 'proper' tea and bags of crisps are one thing but a skinny latte with a cinnamon stick will bring little more than a curled lip, a withering look, and the offer of a cup of weak Nescafe. (Though I have to admit, that over the years, things have improved a little on this front, but then they needed to.)

In order to compensate for the lack of Formosa Oolong tea, and buttered crumpets with Apple & Blackberry preserve in the Station Buffet, there is the Pullman dining train. One of my 'old school' chums went to work on the Pullmans on the Kings Cross, Harrogate services and I myself have, as a result of this happenstance, had several enjoyable meals and journeys in Pullman luxury between Kings Cross and Leeds, when I was a footplateman back in the 1960s, but I digress. The recreation of the past is what it's all about – those good old days when the Bank Manager wore a trilby hat, drove a Daimler or an Armstrong Siddley, and travelled by train in Pullman luxury; they still do, and in lovingly restored Pullman coaches with impeccably uniformed waiters to complete the fantasy. Today you can enjoy Pullman dining as you are hauled around the Surrey hills by No.35028 Clan Line 'one of the regulars' during my time at Nine Elms; an engine I've worked on countless times, well 30 or 40 anyway.

Ex-LNER Class K4 2-6-0, No.61994 The Great Marquess, departing Bewdley – SVR.

'The Train Now Departing', 'Great Railway Journeys' 'Branch line Britain' and a hundred others invite the reader/viewer on a wistful, whimsical, journey across a bucolic Britain of a sort found mainly on jigsaw puzzles and tins of Toffee, usually of a dubious origin. Whimsical journeys may have worked for Alice in Wonderland and the Titfield Thunderbolt but they cut very little ice with accountants or historians. Having said that, there is, in Alice's Adventures, a train ride on which she discovers that; 'even the smoke was worth a thousand pounds a puff' - the railway gravy train even runs in children's stories, so it would seem.

The  photograph, the one above, of No. 61994 The Great Marquess, departing from Bewdley Station, in our peregrination across my railway mindscape, both old and new, contains a number of 'railway' inconsistencies of which the general public or reader  would be utterly unaware, though  the enthusiasts, the 'Gricers' of the title, instantly recognise them. The locomotive in the photograph, which was originally designed by, Sir Nigel Gresley, for the LNER, to run over the 'West Highland' route between Glasgow and Mallaig finished its days hauling coal round Fife. No.61994 The Great Marquess would have been a most unlikely sight on a Great Western Railway secondary line, even after nationalisation.

The departing train, itself a metaphor for that magical mystery tour – the journey through life, has a remarkable life history of its own, but that's another story. The engine is big, black, and smoking, with a hot and sulphurous air – at its heart a blazing fire, regularly stoked, a veritable Hades on wheels. However, if we leave aside the romance for a second, it could just as easily be described as a large piece of recycled industrial machinery, a very minor cog from the vast rail travel machine.

Ex-Lancashire & Yorkshire Railway 0-6-0, No.957, with a vintage train, near Oakworth – K&WVR.

Romantic, symbolic, and metaphoric are every bit as much a part of the railway lexicon as ballast, bullhead, and semaphore, they just do different jobs. Romantic, in the days before package holidays to the Costa Plenty, was two weeks in St.Ives travelling there and back on the Cornish Riviera Express. The, not so, lucky ones enjoyed their romance on evening excursions from any Northern Town of your choice to Blackpool, Bridlington, Cleethorpes, or Scarborough – just time for a paddle in the briny, a pint of foaming ale in the sea front bar, and a bag of fish 'n' chips on the way back to the station. As things hot up in the compartment, on the way home, we cut to the metaphor of the driving wheels and piston rods with all the subtlety of a train crash. In the 50s the sex was always symbolic, a crooked seam here, a smudge of mascara there – and we mustn't forget that 'lipstick on the collar'. 'Full frontal' in the 1950s was, simply, an attack on the Maginot Line!

Romance and railway is cliché of the first magnitude but there are other intangible, elegiac, and esoteric qualities which get rather less of an airing. Railways cross landscapes without roads, across, moors and fells, following river gorges, and on over swathes of countryside only visible from the train. However, many more railway lines emerge from the very bowels of the city, through smoke and soot lined tunnels, over and under blackened bridges, the streets about are all 'on the wrong side of the tracks'. Vast cuttings of brick, factories, goods yards, and then - out into the land of the semi-detached, speed rising in line with the property values. Pistons pound, wheels turn, and the scenery rolls by – but when the railway began its own journey a very different sort of mental mindscape existed in the public consciousness.

Ex-LMS Class 5, No.45407, near Wormit, in Fife, shortly after crossing the Tay Bridge.

For millennia, before the coming of the locomotive age, people's view of their world included the notion that the things in their world were made from various combinations of four elements, earth, air, fire, and water and these ideas were still in common circulation when the steam driven railway opened for business. Steam locomotives, it could be said, embody all these elements. Ores of the earth made into the steel of their frames, or the fires in the firebox, elements of air work their magic in the process of combustion, vaporised water, droplets of steam, the locomotive is the whole alchemical road show on wheels. This produces a rather unusual contrast, steam locomotives were, simultaneously, the foremost technological invention of the age, a product of new scientific theories about the nature of heat, of new forms of metal making and the attendant chemistry; factors such as these, along with new achievements in engineering, used in the locomotive's construction, could be seen as the very antithesis of the 'elemental' world view. Despite its technological brilliance, somehow, the locomotive appealed, to the general public, at least as much, if not more so, on that elemental level.

Ex-BR Class 5 4-6-0, No73129, at Oakworth Station, on the Keighley & Worth Valley Railway.

There is another possible reason why the steam locomotive took the hold on the public consciousness that it undoubtedly did, one with a psychological, almost evolutionary, dimension. In his book the Psychoanalysis of Fire, the French philosopher, Gaston Bachelard, suggests humans have all manner of profound, poetic, visual, and psychological attachments to fire. From the myth of Prometheus to Swan Vestas, Dante's Inferno to the Crazy World of Arthur Brown and his chart topping 'Fire', funeral pyre to living room fire, whichever way you cut it Bachelard has a point – fire has had a very significant influence on human culture and, more importantly, this influence pre-dates recorded history. Our attachment to fire is, in Bachelard's view, connected right back to the very beginnings of 'human' existence and to such psychological factors as fear of the dark, a very real fear in a world full of predators and no illumination. I have been to darkest Africa, well Senegal and the Gambia, and spent nights in the bush, listening to what I can only describe as the sounds of predation – glad not have been on the menu myself. Fire itself was also a threat to the early humans, just as it is today; raging, bush, and forest fires still kill people and destroy crops and property.

Ex-GWR 15xx Class 0-6-0PT, No.1501, near the summit of Eardington bank – SVR.

At the heart of every steam locomotive is a raging fire, ( for the pedants - yes I know there are 'fireless' locomotives), but this is not the destructive devastation of a wild fire it is, rather, a blazing furnace harnessed, by man, to produce an altogether different form of power to be used in pursuit of his own ends. The fire, or more precisely the light it produces, is also a highly visible and recognisable sight when the locomotive is being stoked, and especially so at night or in the dark. Imagine how it must have seemed to the people of the 1830s and 40s, as the dark nights drew in, and they were, for the first time, confronted by the red/orange eerily satanic glows flickering and dancing across the night sky, showers of sparks rising and falling like the passage of some earthly comet, as the train rolled across the landscape from one dark horizon to the next. No surprise that the railways created fright on the one hand and wonder on the other, and especially when one considers the world into which they emerged. A world where candles and oil lamps provided the illumination and street lighting was way-off in the future, a quiet world too, with no blaring hi-fi or TV, no rumbling articulated juggernauts – the noises of the engine and the clattering waggons, coupled to the fast moving flickering glow, must have seemed to have come straight out of Dante's Inferno only to dive back into those subterranean realms moments later – no doubt having collected a few hapless souls along the way.

Tending the blaze is the 'fireman' it is his skill, and at times stamina, which provides the locomotive with its strength and power, if the fire is tended badly the locomotive will, eventually, run out of steam and stop 'for a blow up'. The locomotive has all manner of engineering and physical limitations, they have a theoretical maximum power output and level of adhesion but most of this is meaningless without the addition of the crew. The skill, or lack thereof, on the part of the driver and fireman, their ability to work together as a team is what gives the locomotive its actual capability in the everyday world of moving goods and people from A to B and back. Man and machine in an almost symbiotic relationship, a technological marvel of elemental forces, the steam locomotive is a wonderfully ambiguous artefact. Huge lumps of cold hard metal yet, when they have a fire in their belly they become practically, living, breathing, works of art imbued with a mechanical soul.

Ex-LNER B1 Class 4-6-0, No.61264, at Burrs, on the East Lancashire Railway.

Stations are ambiguous places too – 'how lovely to see you again', 'thank god they're going back'. People filled with expectancy or dread, going on holiday or to the daily grind – did someone mention 'Brief Encounter'? On Saturdays, in post war Britain, throughout the 1950s and well on into the 1960s the ends of station platforms would be full of boys, teenage boys, sitting on porter's barrows or simply hanging around, an Ex-WWII 'respirator pack' slung across their shoulder, note book and pen in hand. Late at night the railway station took on very a different ambience, red signal lights and Taxi signs, kissing couples and noisy revellers – the eerie echo of the station announcer's voice. The inviting yellow glow of the Buffet, mediated by the smell of stewed tea, fags, and stale beer – a peroxide blonde in a badly fitting uniform lolling behind the counter, curled edge sandwiches and cellophane wrapped slices of Dundee cake were what passed for 'Traveller's fare'.

Look again at that photograph of No. 61994 The Great Marquess leaving Bewdley and you will see, leaning from the cab window, the fireman looking directly at the camera – he could be posing. For the footplate crew, perhaps, more than any other railway preservation volunteer occupation, firing the locomotive and driving the train are very much the starring roles. The Fat Controller might run the railway but, the engine driver commands the footplate. It is the driver who grants access to the footplate and the real theatre of the railway – for it is on the footplate and from the footplate that all the drama ensues. Footplatemen are the men who make the black smoke belch or white steam puff, the men who make the wailing whistle scream, in the middle of the night. They're the men with their hands on the levers that control the awesome power of the smoking, fire-breathing, Leviathan – men to whom the passengers must entrust their very lives.

Ex-GWR 28xx Class 2-8-0, No.2807, departing Goathland, on the North Yorkshire Moors Railway.

When steam powered the nation's railway, footplatemen were just 'ordinary' blokes working all hours of the clock, doing a demanding, and frequently dirty, 'blue collar' job - until the early decades of the 20th century they didn't even have the vote. The companies they worked for practically owned them – 'I designed an Automatic Water Scoop Control, patented it and made a Model that was exhibited at the Inventors Exhibition at Westminster Hall. The Railway Co. sacked me for this achievement and informed me that *they employed me Body and Soul*, this I disagreed with. The A.S.L.E & F. took up the case and I was promptly reinstated without loss of pay. (Carter,J.A.

in Moynihan, A. Ed. History of Willesden Branch of A.S.L.E.F. since 1891, unpublished manuscript, p14) Italics added.

Water scoops aside, in the imagination of a great many of those teenage boys hanging around on the platform ends, the engine drivers were legends nonetheless. They drove the locomotives which hauled the 'Talisman' or the 'Golden Arrow', tackled the gradients of wild faraway places like Shap, Whiteball and Drumochter – reality was a little less poetic. Those same teenage boys, almost all of whom never did become footplatemen, are now the men driving the engines on the preserved steam railways – they are also still stalking the platforms – the only change there is that cameras and videos have replaced the respirator packs, notebooks and pens. The dreams of driving an express on the East Coast Mainline and being timed by O.S.Nock never came true – the compensation, for some, is being a part-time engineman on a heritage railway, for the richest few, men like railwayman turned pop-impresario Pete Waterman, owning their very own 'full scale' steam locomotive toy(s).

Ex-BR Britannia Class 4-6-2, No.70013 Oliver Cromwell, pilots Ex-LNER Class K4 2-6-0, No.61994 The Great Marquess, south bound over the summit of Druimauchdar.

Speaking for myself, I enjoyed the best of both worlds, being a platform end enthusiast and a footplateman. I did work services which were timed from the train; my efforts on the footplate did appear as locomotive practice and performance logs in railway enthusiast magazines, and books. And now, just as when I was a schoolboy, I get to hang around the side of railway lines with my camera and write about railways. During my various moves around the railway network which took me from Farnley Jct., via Stewarts Lane and Nine Elms to Holbeck and Wakefield. I worked station pilot at Leeds City Station with Ivatt 2-6-2Ts, and 'The Royal Wessex' and 'Atlantic Coast Express' with Bulleid Pacifics. In my brief spell at Holbeck I worked to Morecambe and to Cleethorpes with Black 5s and B1s respectively, at Wakefield it was coal trains over Copy Pit to Rose Grove and the empties back again with Riddles' Austerities, and Stanier's 8Fs, even fish trains from Hull docks and colliery trip workings down the freight only Dearne Valley line were part of the roster. Mail trains, boat trains, newspaper trains, banana trains, loose coupled trains, fully fitted trains, ballast and engineers' trains, empty coaching stock and the first LCGB 'East Devon Rail Tour' from Waterloo to Exeter and back, I've worked them all. I could write a book about my time on the railway, but there's plenty of old enginemen's tales out there and mine isn't that vastly different to many others who joined the railway in the last decade of steam traction.

Ex-GWR 51xx Class 2-6-2T, No.5164, with a 'local service' departs Bewdley on the Severn Valley Railway.

I worked with men who'd started their own railway careers in the 'Great War' of 1914-1918 and had been drivers and passed firemen in WWII, they'd worked for drivers who began railway service in the 1870s. What we learned as young footplatemen was built on these years of experience, all trains, all weathers, even during bombing raids. I fired for driver Bert Hooker who had, himself, been a fireman in the 1948 Locomotive Exchange Trials. Bert had been on the shovel doing the 'storming Drumochter' bit with a Bulleid light-Pacific whilst I was still in my cradle, but that's enough about me.

The next photograph in our elegiac journey, that of No. 5164, is once again Bewdley station the same as in the photograph of No.61994 The Great Marquess, but with a difference, now the only things which tells you that this picture was taken not in 1936 or 1956 are the clothes being worn by the people on the platform. The branch line connection is just departing, behind No. 5164, and passengers throng the platforms – on platform 1 the mainline train awaits the 'right away' - the entire scene is just that - a scene - a scene of pure railway theatre. Nostalgia you could cut with a knife.

When life in the real world becomes more Hobbesian, (nasty, brutish, and short), by the day it must be a relief, for many, to be able to step back into this idiosyncratic creation of the memory. The real 1936, or 1956 for that matter, was just the same as the real 2010 when this photograph was taken. In 1936 the country was just getting over the 'Great Slump' and in 1956 'Suez', a real line in the sand, dug by Ferdinand de Lesseps, saw our 'brave boys' being sent, by corrupt politicians and vested business interests, to the Middle East to die in the mud – both scenarios still seem horribly familiar as I write.

Perhaps, the picture of No.5164 departing from Bewdley doesn't seem quite so 'chocolate box' after all. The baggage of our own lifetimes will determine which memories are stirred – what the image conjures up in our own minds eye. When I went to this location to take the photograph I had in my mind's eye one of the photographs in R.J.Blenkinsop's book 'Shadows of the Great Western'. This book, Shadows of the Great Western, contains the railway equivalent of the black and white photographs taken of the Hollywood movie stars of the 1950s, and is oozing with the kind of photographs I'd loved to have taken myself.

Ex-LNWR G2 Class 0-8-0, No.49395, near Esk Valley, at the start of the 1:49 climb to Goathland – NYMR.

Blenkinsop's photographs are 'the real thing' everyday trains carrying goods and passengers, holiday makers and commuters, coal and cattle – today all steam railway photography is photographing a shadow theatre – simulacra even – everything looks real enough but none of it is. The strange thing is that the world in general is going in the same direction – 'reality' is reality TV, Big Brother and Dragons Den, the Apprentice and the Only way is Essex. Nobody wants to know about 'nuffink' and surprise, surprise, nobody does. Peterloo – 'never 'eard of it', Tolpuddle, 'yer 'avin' a larf ain't ya.'

In a very real sense the people involved with railway preservation, volunteers and visitors alike, are time travellers journeying back through their own cherished memories to those days spent on the ends of platforms just like these. Drifting back to the days when the world was, for them, a better, simpler, kinder place. Days when bankers were, an engine assisting a train up an incline, and politicians only kissed babies, days when there was no political correctness – especially not the 'gone mad' variety. In this mindscape of sublime summers filled with picnics and fluffy white clouds – there were no hard hats and hi-visibility clothing - Elf and Safety were the names of characters in the Christmas panto.

Ex-LMS Class 5 4-6-0, No.44871, approaching Oakworth, the Railway Children's station, on the K&WVR.

Stations have always been places of escape; escaping from the heat, dirt, and dust of the towns and cities to the country or sea side, escape from the 'everybody knows your business' confines of village life for the anonymity afforded by the city. For some, like the homeless, or the 'bag ladies', and other lost souls, the stations used to be a refuge. Not today's modern 'don't leave your bag unattended', surveillance camera littered station, but places like Waterloo in the 1960s, which I knew at first hand. Waterloo, like many a city centre station, had its share of down and outs – they wore great overcoats stuffed with old newspapers, quarrelled with each other, and scuttled after 'tab' ends. Ah! Those were the days my friends.

Muddying the waters still further is the fact that ever since the dawn of photography and the birth of the moving picture, stations have been film sets just as they are in these photographs and many a heritage line has profited handsomely through being utilised as a back drop in film and television productions.

The Railway Children, the Titfield Thunderbolt, Murder on the Orient Express, and even Oh! Doctor Beeching all have heritage railway connections. The Railway Children a putative 'classic' of British cinema has been a valuable source of income for the Keighley & Worth Valley Railway for 40 years, and, to my certain knowledge, at least one K&WVR society member has dined out long and large on the strength of his very minor acting role in the movie. The North Yorkshire Moors Railway has benefitted enormously from its links with the long running TV series Heartbeat. The once sleepy village of Goathland, where sheep grazed in the street, became the mythic Aidensfield and, almost overnight, became a tourist trap with visiting coach parties and the village shop re-named Aidensfield stores. The sheep have been replaced by the sheeple, herds of wandering 'telly addicts' aimlessly grazing on crisps, ice cream, and take-aways.

Ex-BR Class 4MTT 2-6-4, No.80116, (actually 80072), passing Goathland signal box, on the NYMR.

Look more closely at the picture of No.80116 and you will see, on the platform, on the right, a young boy, with a camera, much as you might have done, in 1960 whatever, when Aidensfield was set. Look to the left of the engine and a piece of real railway theatre is taking place, and an act which must be performed without fault if trains and passengers are to be kept safe. This is no symbolic exchange of tokens, but a very real one, the fireman is passing the signalman the single line token which will enable him to unlock the signals to allow another train into the single line section, in this case between Goathland, (Aidensfield), and Grosmont. Many aspects of railway theatre can be taken fairly loosely but not adherence to the rules of signalling – having two trains travelling in opposite directions on a single line is the stuff of disaster movies or nightmares, not to be duplicated in the 'real' world, not even on a heritage railway! All sorts of little cameos are, or are just about to, happen, the Bobby has his arm out to 'catch' the token, the boy with his camera is set to press the shutter, an elderly porter watches the train move by. The only planned part was an intention to capture the token exchange – seeing that young boy in the shot I took was a lovely bonus, an unexpected window onto my own boyhood days on a station platform – 'spotting trains'.

Ex-SR N15 'King Arthur' Class 4-6-0, No.777 Sir Lamiel, with the TPO, near Loughborough, on the Great Central Railway.

Moving pictures of or from steam hauled trains are amongst some of the earliest moving images ever to be captured anywhere on film. In the 1926 silent movie classic The General, starring Buster Keaton, the real star is the, 'The General', a locomotive, and the movie is loosely based on real events of the American Civil war – the so called 'Great Locomotive Chase'. So, the story goes that during the spring of 1862 a group of Union army volunteers, 'on a daring wartime exploit', stole the Western Atlantic Railway's Rogers, Ketchum & Grosvenor designed 4-4-0, 'The General', in the town of Big Shanty, to the north of Alabama, and set off, hotly pursued by local Confederate troops and railway officers, north towards Chattanooga destroying the tracks and telegraph along the way. Not quite the 'Chattanooga Choo-choo' – which, some 80 years later, became a big wartime hit for Glenn Miller and his orchestra.

Here in Blighty, in 1855, there was the first of the 'Great Train Robberies' – when a large quantity of gold bullion was stolen from a South Eastern Railway train, they know not where, on the journey between London Bridge and Folkestone. And you thought holding up the bullion train only happened in 'cowboy' movies. Many years later Sean, 'you expect me to talk' Connery, as a sort of 'gentleman thief', was the star of a movie loosely based on the events of that May night, in 1855, when gold, en-route to France to pay for the Crimean War, simply 'vanished' – a sort of Victorian 'Goldfinger' in which Bond, sorry Connery, played the baddie. And who can forget engine driver Burt Lancaster steaming around the environs of Paris with a train load of art treasures, in an increasingly desperate bid to prevent them being shipped back to Germany, by the Nazis, in the succinctly titled 'The Train'. Even the Underground, well the New York subway at least, has starred in a movie, the 'high tension', original version, of Taking Pelham 123 with Robert Shaw as the villain.

Ex-GWR 41xx Class 2-6-2T, No. 4160, crossing Dunster marsh, on the WSR, near Minehead.

The Great Locomotive Chase and the Great Train Robbery, whilst they are very different acts and even on different continents, do have something in common – they both became part of the 'mythology of railways'. Real world railway events which became the subjects of movies, just as events in movies in which railways are a feature enter into railway folklore. The classic example of the latter is the faux pas in the Hitchcock version of John Buchan's novel The 39 Steps in which we see the hero on a train bound for Scotland followed by footage of a Great Western Railway express bursting out of the famous 'Box Tunnel' on the Paddington to Bristol route. A great example of the former comes from the Ealing Comedies version of the Belles of St.Trinians and their 'comic' interpretation of the Great Locomotive Chase, filmed, ironically, on the Longmoor Military Railway. There's even a distant echo of the Great Locomotive Chase in one of Wallace and Gromit's adventures, The Wrong Trousers, in which Wallace, Gromit and Feathers McGraw, ( a diamond stealing penguin who disguises himself as a chicken by sticking a rubber glove on his head –mmm!), have a bizarre 'model' railway chase around Wallace's house.

Ex-BR 2-10-0, No. 92220 Evening Star, (actually No.92214), with a demonstration freight working, near Loughborough, on the Great Central Railway.

In the interests of science trains have been crashed head on into each other and filmed, they've even filmed crashes involving flasks of nuclear waste being carried by rail – to ensure the flasks were well enough constructed that in the event of accident they didn't break open and irradiate us all. Cameras have been placed on and under the locomotives, in the track, and have been flown overhead in planes and helicopters, from Zeppelins and hot air balloons too, for all I know. In more recent times trains and locomotives have been filmed and used to sell wall paper paste, Coca Cola, M&S food and fashion ranges, biscuits, and who knows what to who knows whom – the railway preservationists made valuable income from them all, all except the crashing head on with nuclear flasks bit that is.

Photographers, Admen, and movie makers were not the only artists with a penchant for capturing and manipulating the railway station or railway landscape. In 1870s Paris, Monet painted a whole series of wonderful impressionist images of the Gare St. Lazare, the 'Derriere' of which, the Gare St.Lazare's not Monet's, became one of the legendary photographer, Henri-Cartier Bresson's, most celebrated images. Here in Britain JWM Turner, in the early 1840s, painted his evocative impression of a steam locomotive crossing Maidenhead viaduct, at speed, in the rain – even the tortured genius Vincent van Gogh painted pictures with steam trains in them.

A lone passenger awaits the train, at Staverton Station, on the South Devon Railway.

The drama of the railway station captured the imaginings of other artistic souls, Poets as well as Painters, and one of this Nation's favourite poems is about a country station on a warm summer afternoon – Edward Thomas' Adlestrop. 'Yes. I remember Adlestrop …' the timeless image of timelessness that Thomas conjures up in Adlestrop is the very life blood of the 'heritage' railway line. Country stations where the volunteer's plant flowers and sell homemade cakes, feature at practically every heritage line – the best of them win prizes and tourism awards. Whilst it may be fair to say that during the early post-war years some country stations had a bucolic air and some won prizes for their flower beds and hanging baskets, for a great many travellers, they were the exceptions rather than the norm.

Not all poets were enthusiasts of the country station or even railways and some, like the 'lonely cloud', Wordsworth, who vociferously 'railed' against the railway's arrival in his daffodil watching haunts in the Lake District, were the forerunners of our modern-day NIMBY; a, generally speaking, objectionable social group who seem to have little purpose in life other than to say no - or yes if it's hunting defenceless animals with packs of slavering dogs, and leaving the EU.

Ex-LMS Royal Scot Class 4-6-0, No.46115 Scots Guardsman, alongside the river Tay, on the main line at West Ferry, near Dundee, en route to Inverness, via Aberdeen.

Almost a hundred years after Wordsworth's condemnation of all things railway, in the 1930s, another wordsmith, W. H. Auden, wrote what is, possibly, the definitive railway poem – the Night Mail. Written by Auden to accompany a film about the activities of the Travelling Post Office – the 'Night Mail' became one of the gems of British documentary film-making and poetry alike. The cadences of Auden's poem are based on the rhythms of an accelerating locomotive until the final verse when the rhythm slows, mirroring the actual journey. In one of those little quirks of fate, the engine which featured in the 1936 film, the then un-rebuilt Royal Scot class 4-6-0 No.(4)6115 Scots Guardsman, is one of two of the class of 70 rebuilt versions which survived the mass extinctions of the 1960s, the other being the doyen of the class No.(4)6100 Royal Scot – actually No.(4)6152 The Kings Dragoon Guardsman – a switch of name plates fully intended to deceive.

Leaving aside crafty name swapping and the poetic images of rural railway bliss in a time that never, actually, existed outside of artistic license or imagination, the station has a murkier, less rose tinted aspect. Stations are frontiers as much in a social as a geographical sense; it is not only the ticket barrier one needs to pass through, class barriers too have to be negotiated. Stations were places where, before the age of the motor car, the rich, to their distaste, would be obliged to rub shoulders with the not so rich – class was everywhere, first, third or Pullman. So important were these distinctions, and so well adhered to, that separate waiting rooms enforced the 'social apartheid' – a little anecdote about the famous locomotive engineer Patrick Stirling neatly encapsulates the issue. In the Railway News of November 1895 the author of Patrick Stirling's obituary commented that; '...nor had he [Stirling] much sympathy for such new-fangled ideas as bogie carriages and third class lavatories'. The less well to do, it seems, would simply have to 'contain' themselves.

Having entered the station we purchased our 'passages' and had our luggage 'portered' before 'boarding', (a distinctly nautical, if not piratical, turn of phrase), the train - even a few native bearers wouldn't seem out of place in this section of the railway lexicon. Once on board the train, the passenger simply became the raw material in a vast travel machine. The writer, philosopher, and opium eater, Thomas De Quincy wrote beautifully of the essential difference between travelling in a stage coach or a railway one. 'Seated in the old mail-coach, we needed no evidence out of ourselves to indicate the velocity. ... The vital experience of the glad animal sensibilities made doubts impossible on the question of our speed; we heard our speed, we saw it, we felt it as a thrilling; and this speed was not the product of blind insensate agencies, that had no sympathy to give, but was incarnated in the fiery eyeballs of the noblest among brutes, in his dilated nostril, spasmodic muscles, and thunder-beating hoofs.' (De Quincy's comments were first published in Blackwood's Magazine during 1849, but the quote is taken from Wolfgang Schivelbusch's The Railway Journey: The Industrialisation of Time and Space in the 19th Century)

Ex-SR B-o-B Class 4-6-2, No.34070 Manston, near the summit of Eardington bank – SVR.

The journey from stage coach to railway carriage isn't simply one of pace it is, as De Quincy so poetically describes, an altogether different sensation, physically, mentally, visually, and audibly. Seated in the railway carriage, which at the outset was likely to be little more than an open wagon with seats, the early railway traveller undertook a transmutation of time and distance of previously un-dreamed of rapidity. The distance moved over, (ever decreasing amounts of), time elapsed became the unique selling point of the railway travel machine and a major source of interest for a great many railway enthusiasts to this day. How far and how fast had its first official public outing at the Rainhill trials in 1829 and from that point on all manner of people, from the pulpit to Grubb Street, became involved in recording locomotive practice and performance – it certainly didn't begin with O.S. Nock – he was simply one of the more prominent exponents of logging locomotive performance in the 1950s.

Once the iron horse began to supplant the animal version as the nation's preferred mode of transportation, the Industrial Revolution really started picking up pace; speeds rose from the 10mph to 15mph of the early engines like, Locomotion No.1, the Steam Elephant, or Trevithick's 'Catch me who can', ('Catch me who can' was a kind of steam locomotive hauled fairground ride set up not far from what was to become, thirty years later, Euston Station), to the giddy heights of the 29mph set by Rocket at Rainhill. The nay-sayers were predicting that if you travelled at speeds in excess of 30mph you would suffocate – strangely no-one did and, by 1850, speeds of almost 80mph were being claimed for engines on Brunel's broad gauge (7' gauge) and over on the London North Western, Webb's Precursor class 2-4-0 No. 790 Hardwicke claimed 90mph during the famous Railway Races to the North in 1895.

Ex-GWR Castle Class 4-6-0, No.5029 Nunney Castle, at Moorgates – NYMR.

This 'quest for speed' has still not abated even though conventional railed trains, here in Britain, can now run up to 186mph on the high speed channel tunnel route, speeds on the Continent and in Japan and China are even higher. However, speeds are not the issue with heritage lines, almost the opposite in fact. Though one might argue that travelling from 2014 to 1950 something in the time it takes to walk from the station car park to the station booking hall is pretty rapid transit, albeit retrograde motion.

Real railway stations of the 1950s, on which the vast majority of heritage lines base their 'timeless images', were frequently run down, drab, grey, and depressing places, for many travellers they still are, glazing missing from platform awnings, locked and boarded waiting rooms – vandalised benches – the staff were axed and then the lines. (Carnforth Station, which starred in Brief Encounter was, like the film, typical for the period a dreary and draughty place where the platforms were connected via flights of stone stairs and a damp, badly lit, underpass – it was all too easy to get 'smut in your eye'.) The real villains of the piece however, were those members of the political and business class responsible for wrecking and undermining the railway network, more often than not, to serve their own ill-gotten business, political, and/or financial interests.

Ex-LNER Class J72 0-6-0, No.69023, departing Hampton Loade Station – SVR.

There's been no shortage of erudition and claptrap about how, after the war, the railways were not sexy enough and how the growth of private car ownership, was another nail in the coffin, but the simple truth is that in the years immediately following Nationalisation the railways were put first under the management of a career Civil Servant and then a demobbed General, both of whom were, in business terms, out of their depth and clueless as to how the war ravaged railways should move forward. If you throw in a cadre of indolent and visionless petty bureaucrats and leaven with a sprinkling of junior management jobsworths you're well on the road to stifling initiative, and a sure-fire way to run down any business is to drive out all 'enterprise'.

There are also issues surrounding coal and iron ore mining, as well as the steel making business, which are not un-related to the train wreck that the railways became – successive post-war governments have a great many skeletons in the closet marked 'botched railway / industrial planning' from Margam to Whitemoor and one shoddy and badly designed diesel locomotive to the next – some, like the 'Warships', averaged less than 80 miles between failures. The braking systems on some diesel multiple units were so poor that where you stopped could be a bit of a lottery, a nightmare to drive. Drivers who worked on the 'Peak' class Sulzers used to take a blanket to work to keep warm in the cab and the drivers of the Deltics, (the rising stars of the ECML and the successors to Gresley's record setting A4s), were given ear protectors because of the fearful racket the engines made and one can add to this the constant stink of diesel. (The 'ear protectors' were just wax plugs – no expense spared on the 'modern' new railway.) While we're on the subject of expenses the railway's former shareholders continued to receive dividend payments until well into the 1960s despite the putative 'loss-making' of the 'Nationalised' British Railways.

Ex-LMS Class 2MT 2-6-0, No. 46521, with a demonstration mineral train, near Loughborough – GCR.

Many bemoan the loss of the Somerset & Dorset line where rural stations did have hanging flower baskets, and 'chocolate box' names; names like Midsomer Norton, Sturminster Newton and the unforgettable Evercreech Junction. However, just before you become all dewy eyed over the loss of the idyllic S & D route spare a thought for the former Manchester Sheffield & Lincoln Railway's 'Woodhead' route between Manchester and Sheffield. Building the Woodhead route was a titanic struggle between man the Pennines, and the elements, which lasted not for days, or weeks, but years. Scores of men died building the line and particularly during construction of the tunnel section under the Pennines, their wives and children died too, not from injury but from typhoid and cholera – a direct result of the crude conditions under which they existed. No accommodation was provided

Ex-GWR 56xx Class 0-6-2T, No. 6695, with a demonstration freight, near Hampton Loade – SVR.

by the company, or the contractor, and so the men built whatever shelter they could from whatever they could find to hand on the moors. Constructing the first Woodhead tunnel took 7 long years and the navvies with their kith and kin lived in crude shelters almost throughout - one newspaper report of the time said they were living in, 'near godless savagery'. So great was the overall loss of life during the building of the Woodhead tunnel that a parliamentary inquiry was held into the causes of the high death rates; George Stephenson, amongst others, was called as a witness. To sum up the enquiry, read – 'you want the railways, it's a risky business, and it's inevitable that people will die'. There was no sick pay, no death benefits, no 'workman's compensation' – only the maimed and the grieving remained. The future prospect for the survivors or the wives and children of those killed was in one or other of the fearful hell holes known as 'the workhouse'.

This line across the 'backbone' of England, a route which, in later years, over part of its length had a highly efficient electrification system in place, and linked two of northern England's largest cities, was closed, almost overnight, with barely a whisper. These were the days - these were the days when you wondered what was going on, which track was the gravy train on now? The utter lack of foresight, strategic planning, or anything even resembling a coherent transport policy stands as a constant indictment of the corrupt practices of the political classes and their spiv chums in the city.

Nationalised Railways, or any other Nationalised industry for that matter, were never going to be allowed to work when, within three years of their inception, the country was being governed by a political party implacably opposed to seeing nationalisation succeed on any level. The writing was all over the wall when a man whose business was building roads and motorways rose through the ranks to become Minister of Transport – yes Ernest Marples, aka 'minister for motorways', and not a conflict of interest in sight! All that mattered then was then. Oh! And 'loadsa money'. Off in the distance a voice cried – 'and what about all those trams', trams sent to their doom by the London Rubber Company and the greed, vanity, and short-sighted stupidity of local councils / councillors the length and breadth of Britain – many of whom are now trying, at colossal expense, to re-install some form of tramway system?

Bagnall 0-4-0ST, Kent No.2, departs from the former NCB Dilhorne Colliery sidings, on the Foxfield Railway, with a train of mineral empties.

(Ernest Marples, one half of the Marples / Ridgeway construction group which built parts of the M1 and the Hammersmith flyover, amongst other things. Despite being appointed Minister of Transport, Marples, continued to hold, by fair means or foul, his shareholdings in Marples Ridgeway which was contrary to Parliamentary rules – even back in the 1950s. He fled the country in 1975, shifting his assets to Monaco and Liechtenstein, to avoid paying the 30 years of back taxes he owed, he was also sued by the tenants of the slum properties he owned and failed to maintain – all in all a really charming 'self-made' Tory gentleman and railway wrecker.)

Back in the 19th Century novel features of the newly invented rail travel machine, as with almost any 'new technology' bubble, provided the unscrupulous with hitherto un-dreamed of opportunities for all manner of fraud and chicanery. So rife was 'insider trading' in shares in British Railway companies, in the late 19th Century, that, at one point, French traders withdrew from the market altogether. Railway construction and travel didn't just create new ways to liberate the gullible from their wealth it revolutionised the view of the landscape whilst simultaneously changing that landscape forever, the mental one every bit as much as the physical one.

Ex-GWR 14xx Class 0-4-2T, No.1450, alongside Northwood lane, near Bewdley - SVR.

The railway had a major hand in breeding many new and innovative forms of commerce; transforming the manufacturing of locomotives from the work of skilled artisans 'crafting' every individual nut, screw, washer, and bolt to something akin to 'Standard Whitworth' – creating machinery to produce identical parts time after time just as Whitworth had done with threads for nuts and bolts, machines and locomotives were now made by machines. Standardised, machine made, parts were an important feature in the growing success of the railway: this form of manufacture further accelerated the division of labour, already being used with some success in the dark and satanic mills, by the time the railways started their expansion. Such was the railway's need for standardisation that not even time escaped its clutches.

In order to make a network of inter-connecting services operate effectively time-tabling was vital and in order to achieve this end out went the ages old 'local time' based on sunrise times and in came 'Railway' time. Clocks were all made to tell the same time; some said it was to make the trains more punctual - to make them 'run on time' – actually it was to allow a realistic timetable to be drawn up, one in which arrivals and departures would be timed to GMT whether they were in Carmarthen or Clacton. I remember once hearing a wonderful radio play on this very topic – 'Time added on' was the title and I believe James Bolam played a leading role. Someone, I forget who, once said, 'Radio is the theatre of the mind, TV is the theatre of the mindless', and in this particular instance this was very true.

Ex-LSWR 0298 Class 0-4-2T, No. 30585, with a demonstration 'china clay' working, at Boscarne Junction, on the Bodmin & Wenford Railway.

In creating new ways to see the world, through the window of a speeding train, by changing the equation between time and distance, by replacing the generations old 'local time' with 'railway time' the railway was akin to the 17th century Alchemist, transforming not only base metals into machines but altering the very social fabric itself. These effects, cultural, social, mechanical, and even metaphorical, produced by the arrival of the railway spread, like treacle on a butty – there were those wags who even went so far as to suggest that in some rural areas it lessened the degree of inbreeding.

Railways, however, didn't cease their creation of the identical when they made machines with standardised parts or organised the clocks to tell 'railway time', they wanted a uniform(ed) workforce too – a 'standard' porter in Basingstoke indistinguishable from and interchangeable with one from Waterloo or Crewe, or put another way the workforce were simply to be considered as machines too. Ordered and orderly workers presenting a positive company image, dependable servants in smart livery, trustworthy and upstanding – just like the footmen, or doormen, that the railway's proprietors were accustomed to dealing with. Speaking of which, at the other end of that snaking social ladder increasing numbers of the Members of both Lords and Commons owned railway shares, held railway directorships and cross board memberships – a spiders web of conflicts of interest, self-interest and down-right pomposity. Heritage Railways too are not short of the ennobled, the 'Squirarchy'/ Great and Good, not to mention the pompous, amongst their Patrons or on their boards – maybe just coincidence. Perhaps, they're the ones with time on their hands trying to avoid the 'devil's work' or should that be avoiding 'working like the devil' – a term the employees were rather more familiar with.

Ex-LMS Class 3F 0-6-0, No.47406, 'light engine', and Gricer, near Loughborough, on the GCR.

By now any trainspotter worth his salt will be telling you that the railway journey really begins not at the station but at the shed or, to give it its Sunday name, the Motive Power Depot, where the crew sign on duty to prepare the engine which will pull the train taking the passengers on their journey. Engine sheds, which one author somewhat poetically described as 'cathedrals of steam', would be, on the same line of reasoning, the Mecca of spotterdom. Some sheds, like Kings Cross, for example, were legendary in status because of the trains they supplied motive power for and the names of some of the crews who worked there. Others enjoyed a different kind of status, sheds like Copley Hill in Leeds, at the opposite end of the line from Kings Cross, was famously difficult to 'bunk' - that is to get around without being thrown out or escorted from the premises by the railway police.

Former Turkisk Railways, Stanier 8F 2-8-0, No.45160, at Loughborough MPD on the GCR.

Sheds, to a great many of those teenage boys from the platform ends, were a challenge, a rite of passage, 'trespass forbidden' read the signs – a form of words which could have been lifted straight from the Ten Commandments. Clive Groome, like myself, an ex-footplateman, wrote, in his excellent book about the footplatemen, their origins and status, 'The Decline and Fall of the Engine Driver', that the footplatemen were a Clan – if they were, then the shed was their ancestral home. Sheds were where you could get up close and personal with the engines themselves and, possibly, meet and talk to those 'Clansmen', the real heroes - the engine drivers. Being 'off limits' the Shed was, on many levels, an alien environment; a place where pools of iridescent, oil streaked, water could be illuminated by shafts of sunlight pouring through broken sections of roof, whilst in pits under the engines fitters toiled by the light of tallow or 'flare' lamps, ( a form of illumination which would have been quite familiar to people living in Biblical times).

Ex-BR 9F 2-10-0, No.92214, being oiled and watered, at Grosmont MPD, on the NYMR.

 On shed, which came in two main variants, the running shed, and the round house, the engines stood in circles or rows, some cold and silent, others gently hissing, wisps of steam drifting from their injector pipes or the cylinder drain cock. Sheds, and especially the big ones, were the 'shock and awe' of train spotting. Guided tours of Crewe or Derby works on an open day, or visiting Doncaster Plant with a works pass, were spectacular but lacked the frisson provided by 'bunking' a shed with a reputation for being a difficult place to bunk round.

Travelling around the country and trying to 'bunk' the sheds was a regular weekend pastime for bands of dedicated spotters, and not always with a valid ticket. A regular wheeze for some, me included, was to journey from Leeds to Doncaster or to York on a platform ticket, I suspect that many other stations and destinations were visited in this manner by bands of dedicated rail fans all over the country. A major factor in the heritage railways being what they are today is because what has been preserved wasn't the adult world of rents and mortgages to pay, jobs to go to and meals to cook; but the world of Combined Volumes, works passes, what would be on the 4 o'clocker, the platform end of a mainline station circa 1959 and the belief, amongst some, that challenging accepted wisdom and authority was not only a fun thing to do it could also produce worthwhile results.

Ex-GWR 28xx Class 2-8-0, No.3850, ready for duty, at Bishops Lydeard MPD, on the WSR.

The world of the platform end and the shed bash was a world with its own language of Dub Dees and Semis, Derby 4s, (known to some footplatemen as 'Night Fighters'), Bongos, Streaks, Packets, and even Flying Pigs and many, many, more – cops were previously unseen locomotives not the constable Dibble variety. This was a time when a whole day of fun and entertainment cost no more than the price of a platform ticket and a bike or bus ride to the station and back. A time when all day Saturday could go by alongside the railway with pencil, paper, a couple of cheese and beetroot sandwiches, and all swilled down with orange squash or a bottle of Tizer.

Surprisingly there's even a degree of education involved in these platform end gatherings - certainly an element of knowing the answers to 'pub quiz' questions. 'Namers', such as Royal Scots or Jubilees, taught you the names of the provinces of India and Canada or the Colonial states in Africa, India or the West Indies alongside those of Admirals of the Fleet from the days of Nelson's navy to that of WW I – Royal Scots added to this melange with the names of regiments from the British Army. Everything and everyone from the Kings of England and water fowl, through species of antelope, stars in the heavens, the names of shires and counties, football teams and fox hunts could all be found within the covers of the Combined Volume. For those erudite enough to know about such matters one could add the names of Greek or Roman gods and goddesses – for the plebeians there were the Derby winners. Silly me I forgot that horse racing was the 'sport of Kings', the plebs just lost their shirts. (The Combined Volume was a book with a list of all the locomotives in service with British Railways, including the names of those which had them.)

A contrast in chimneys, Ex-GWR Hall Class 4-6-0, No.4936 Kinlet Hall, 'on shed' at Bridgnorth MPD – SVR.

When it came to dishing out names it wasn't just the big express engines which received them, shunting engines, and locomotives on industrial railways, far from public gaze, were given names too. Clearly naming locomotives wasn't simply something dreamed up by fanciful Victorian Admen, to draw in the punters. If what was needed was a means of simple identification then all that was required was a number – but from the outset names were bestowed. Lathes, looms, and stationary boilers weren't given names so why name steam locomotives – did naming them in some way humanise them? Did giving locomotives names imply status or make them less scary to a wary public?

We may never know why engines were named, but what we can say is that they were regarded, by the public, very differently from other types of industrial machinery if for no other reason than by virtue of the fact that they considered them important enough to give them individual names. With names such as Novelty, Rocket, and Sans Pareil or even Puffing Billy and Locomotion No.1 you can see a correspondence between the name and the object. It requires no leap of imagination to be able to picture Flying Scotsman or Thunderer hurtling along the permanent way – they sound like steam locomotive names. The thing is though; names like Flying Scotsman and Thunderer are quite rare, many, many more engines have utterly inappropriate names. Take, for instance, the London North Western Railway Lady of the Lake or 'Problem' class 2-2-2s there was, well, the eponymous 'Problem' and 'Eunomia', or take the Billington's E4 class 0-6-2T 'Stoat's Nest' or the Stroudley 0-4-2 No. 309 'Splugen' none of which conjure up the sight, sound, or smells, of a 'majestic steam locomotive'. Naming both locomotives and trains did, in time, become an essential part of the 'promotional' activities of the railway companies a practice which has now reached the point where the privatised National railways will put the name of your choice, within reason, on the side of the locomotive, for an appropriate fee naturally.

Ex-GWR 'City' Class 4-4-0, No.3440 City of Truro, on a brake van ride freight, at the Llangollen Railway.

There is a philosophical school of thought which suggests that by conferring names on objects, we are, in one sense, bringing them into existence. In this view naming is a kind of power, in some way it helps create an appearance of permanence about what was, before it was named, simply a 'thing'. Giving things a number de-humanises them, (remember Patrick McGoohan in the television series the Prisoner and 'I'm not a number'), most people remember names more easily than we remember numbers – though many a Gricer can cite name and number for entire classes of named locomotives. Naming the locomotives might also have helped to 'protect' them – thrashing a recalcitrant clack valve with a 7/8th Whitworth spanner might not have been so easy if the engine's name was 'Primrose' or Princess somebody or other! Certainly nobody takes the 7/8th Whitworth spanner to a sticking clack on any of the pampered pets on today's heritage railway.

However, what was named and what wasn't tells a very familiar story - there wasn't a 'Chartist', 'Suffragette', or 'Tolpuddle Martyr' no 'Peterloo' or 'Durham Miner' – 'working class heroes' were exceedingly thin on the ground when it came to naming engines – but then it wasn't the working class who were choosing the names, indeed they played no part whatsoever in either the choice of name or whether the engine even had one. From my own railway experience I can say, without fear of contradiction, that some engines which did not have names did get called names, many of which are, to coin a phrase 'unrepeatable in polite society'. I have also seen engines with names written on in chalk – so obviously some members of the working class did give names, usually affectionate ones in these cases, to the engines they worked on.

Ex-LB&SCR A1X Class 0-6-0, No.662, (once named Martello), with a brake van ride train on the G&WSR.

No one questions the fact that institutions, causes, figures, and heroes created by and drawn from the British working classes will be either under represented or, much more likely, simply ignored at all levels within putative 'polite society' or, as they are sometimes referred to, the 'chattering and political classes' - so it is no surprise that the names of men and women who fought to gain the vote, or create institutions which benefitted their fellows, never made it onto locomotive name plates – nor did they aspire or expect to. If there is a relationship between naming and power there is no doubt where that power resides in the naming of locomotives. Power and motive, motive power, sometimes the relations between these things operates below the conscious level, which tales are retold and reinforced, which ones simply slip into oblivion. His (story) not Her (story), Waterloo not Peterloo,

Christian Martyrs not Tolpuddle ones – little wonder that John Lennon in his song 'Working Class Hero' sang, 'first you must learn how to smile as you kill if you want to live like the folks on the hill'. During the early industrial revolution the working class had very little to smile about and plenty of them met un-timely and un-necessary deaths.

Ex-SR Schools Class 4-4-0, No925 Cheltenham, departs from Quorn & Woodhouse station on the GCR.

One thing you probably wouldn't discover on a visit to a heritage railway or railway museum was that one of the first uses by the State, of the fledgling railway system, was to move troops from the South, using the London & Birmingham, Grand Junction and Liverpool & Manchester Railways, to put down, by force, the Chartists. (So unpopular was this manoeuvre that the troops were forced to march across London, to the station, with their bayonets drawn.) Poor folk demanding the right to a vote wasn't a popular occupation in late 1830s Britain, when Railway Barons like George Hudson or railway builders like Joseph Locke bought 'rotten boroughs' to gain their seats in Parliament. 80 years later, in the early decades of the 20th century, the Suffragettes were still fighting for votes for women. Today half, or more, of the population have no idea that their forebears were put to the sword, beaten, and imprisoned for demanding the right to vote for their own representation in Parliament. In this 'modern age' we have votes for all but barely half of the electorate participate – such hard won rights so easily dismissed and forgotten.

Ex-BR Class 4MTT 2-6-4, No.80002, slipping badly, departs the engineers yard at Oakworth – K&WVR.

Those long-ago, happy, carefree, days spent on the platform end helped to foster other useful sets of social skills, knowledge sharing and social co-operation to name but two of them. Platform end conversations were often about who'd seen what and where and especially the details of any 'foreign engines' on local sheds – particularly rare examples could lead to a mass exodus from the station to the shed in question, replete with mass trespass on arrival. Perhaps, I should add to the learning experience, a healthy dose of scepticism towards arbitrary authority, of 'By order' written on signs, and anyone shouting 'Oy You!'

By contrast, the railway itself was a very 'ordered' environment – there was a rule for everything and footplatemen carried their copy of the company rule book with them – that was a rule too. Knowing and acting upon the rules could mean the difference between life and death for the passengers as well as the crew. In general, Gricers know all manner of esoteric details about the railways from locomotive liveries to carriage designs but they know very little about the rule book nor, for that matter, do they really care – for the Gricer the railways were primarily, and they still are, places of entertainment. What is more is that it was a form of entertainment which had a degree of rule breaking built into it. The major difference between the platform end in the 1950s & 60s and those of today is that on the end of the platform today 'sticking to the rules' is the new norm for railway visitors and workers alike. Bunking preserved railway sheds, en masse, is practically unthinkable even for the most ardent of today's Gricers. Lineside trespass and 'shed bashing' is now regulated by permits, rather like fishing, and all the photographs in this book, which have been taken from lineside locations, have been under this permit system.

Ex-BR Class 4MT 2-6-0, No.76084, and a fine array of signals, at Loughborough, on the Great Central Railway.

The ordering of the railway environment did not spring fully formed from some ancient fount of wisdom but grew out of working practices and methods on the one hand and in response to mishaps and disasters on the other. This organic form of growth applied just as much to the social organisation of the railway staff as it did to the 'engineering' of the railway. In the words of Norman McKillop, (for many years a top link driver at Haymarket and a regular contributor to the Locomotive Journal, under the pseudonym Toram Beg), 'it was not uncommon for junior levels of management to treat those under them with a level of discipline bordering on brutality'. In addition to the long hours of duty, and a 6 ½ day week workers could be fined, or suspended from duty, (with loss of pay), or placed on lower paid work. When you consider that the railways employed, at their height, more than 700,000 people, mostly in blue collar or minor office work you begin to see what made these vast undertakings possible – draconian levels of discipline on the one hand and fear of the work house on the other.

(McKillop also wrote the Lighted Flame, a history of ASLEF, and he found the time to be an active and senior member of the Scottish TUC. Some of his contributions to the ASLEF journal really bring home the dreadful working conditions and pay rates of railwaymen, and the footplatemen in particular, throughout the 1930s, 40s, and into the early 50s.)

The disciplined, uniformed staff, employed by the railway companies in the last quarter of the 19th Century formed a body of men bigger than the army and navy combined and the duties they undertook ranged from greasing points to making artificial limbs. (The London & North Western Railway made prosthetics for members of their staff injured on duty). That these things happened is not happenstance because for the railways to succeed it was not only necessary to create new forms of machines and technologies to deal with the operational requirements of the ever expanding railway system it was also necessary to create a workforce capable of safely operating the rail travel machine itself. Unlike the factory, or mine, where the owner could directly oversee both workforce and capital equipment the railway required new relations between the employer, employee, and the capital equipment they were operating.

Ex-LMS 8F 2-8-0, No.48476, (actually 48305), entering Loughborough, with a mixed freight – GCR.

Machine wrecking was a serious worry for the early capitalists and there is some evidence to suggest that Luddites, or Luddite sympathisers, attempted to wreck trains on Brandling's Colliery Railway as early as 1811. Preventing damage to and destruction of their capital equipment was a very real and serious concern for the early industrialists and railways were not immune from this form of protest by those who objected to industrialisation.

Different companies used different methods to achieve the sort of relationship between their employees and the machinery under their control that would see their expensive equipment treated properly. In the case of the footplatemen this sometimes occurred in the form of one or two crews being given a quasi-ownership of 'their' engine. By these means they were persuaded to 'care' for the equipment they were given to work with. A third element alongside the military levels of discipline and 'quasi-ownership' was the creation of a 'public service ethos' and to compliment this a strong sense of 'company loyalty' – a feature which still exists both on the modern, and the heritage, railway. Intercompany rivalry might have begun in the boardroom and been motivated solely by profit but, at the level of the employees it was not unlike the rivalry between one set of football supporters and another – and there was, most definitely, a hooligan fringe. Trains and locomotives were kidnapped and held to ransom; tracks were dug up leaving whole trains marooned. In the summer of 1852 Midland Railway men seized a Great Northern Railway locomotive in Nottingham which they held for seven months – and this was not an isolated incident.

Ex-GNR 0-6-2T, No.1744, with a single teak coach, at Beck Hole, on the North Yorkshire Moors Railway.

In the years before railway mania many footplate crews, on railways such as the Liverpool & Manchester Railway or the Leicester & Swanington, were handpicked for their posts by George Stephenson himself from men who he knew from his days in the collieries. (At the Liverpool & Manchester Railway's opening day ceremony Stephenson, father and son, along with their assistant Joseph Locke, were amongst those taking control on the footplate of trains in the cavalcade. Locke went on to rival Stephenson in the railway engineering business and was largely responsible for the LSWR mainline from London to Southampton. Locke was a Barnsley lad and the town has a public park named in his honour.) This is one possible reason why many early footplate crews, especially on those lines which Stephenson senior and junior were involved with, came from the colliery railways of North-East England. Once the country was in the grip of 'railway mania' the demand for new railwaymen was such that the railway companies were left with little choice but to recruit from the areas into which they were expanding. This body of men was drawn, in the main, from a population which had, hitherto, been largely rural and agricultural, men more used to timing things by the season or the phases of the moon than the hands of a pocket watch or station clock. Now their lives would be governed by a different rhythm.

Ex-LMS Class 3F 0-6-0T, No.47279, with a short goods, passing 'the mound', near Oakworth – K&WVR.

Rhythm and railway, like bacon and eggs, go really well together and the 'rhythm of the rails' is a relatively hackneyed phrase, much like the lyrics of many a pop song. Why you can almost hear the 'runaway train rattlin' down the line' – though not of course on today's railway of all welded rail, clickety clack, has clacked its last on the clicketyless national network. There are so many genres of music which have warbled, wailed, and crooned about railways, rail travel, the hardships of railway life, and the heroics of railway workers it is hard to know where to begin. There are songs of railway construction from 1880s America, 'Drill Ye Tarriers Drill' – allegedly a reference to the Irish workers who drilled the rock ready for the explosive charges to be placed. In similar vein, also from the

'New World' is 'John Henry' the tale of an African-American who pitted himself against a steam driven hammer and won – only to die from his heroic effort. Closer to home there's the Ballad of John Axon. John Axon was a driver from Stockport (Edgeley) who, in 1957, died on the footplate, in heroic circumstances. Axon died trying, in a cab filled with scalding steam, to slow the progress of Stanier 8F No.48188 as it ran away, with an un-fitted freight, down the 1/58 incline, from Dove Holes Jct. to Chapel-en-le-Frith, following a catastrophic brake failure caused by the severing of the steam supply to the engine brake. Driver Axon was posthumously awarded the George Cross for his bravery.

Ex-GWR 28xx Class 2-8-0, No.2807, with a demonstration ballast train, near Bishops Lydeard, on the West Somerset Railway.

'It takes a lot to laugh it takes a train to cry', according to Bob Dylan who was also rather fond of the sound of 'the South bound whistle of a South bound train'. And almost anyone from South of the Mason-Dixon Line, and Bob Dylan, sang 'the freight train blues'. Songs have coupled the devil to down-bound trains and more than one Country and Western singer was determined to 'go to heaven on a streamlined train'. 50s British rock 'n' roller Lonnie Donegan, made a hit here in the UK, with a song popularised by the American blues legend Leadbelly, 'Rock Island line' – which, it seems, originated in Arkansas State prison. Casey Jones, meanwhile, was heading for disaster with the Cannon Ball Express – Casey was killed trying to stop his train colliding with a stationary goods train – not unlike John Axon, having ordered his fireman to jump he stayed with his engine till the last.

Jukebox records wailed about the trains that took your baby away or brought her back, and when modernity came to Britain, (if it ever has), Don Lang's 6.05 Special was the first 'top of the pops' style show to be broadcast on BBC television – 'Time to jive to the old six five' was its catch phrase and the opening credits rolled over film footage, some of which appeared to be pre-nationalisation era, of steam at work on the West Coast Mainline and crossing the Forth Bridge. Any claims in the lyrics to be, 'right on time', applied only to the fact that it went out at 6.05p.m. on Saturday, not even Mussolini could have made British Railways run to time, well not more than about 85% of the time. Other musical railway 'specials' include the; 'midnight special' a train which took loved ones to that great engine shed in the sky and the 'orange blossom special' which was a popular train with the inmates of Folsom Prison – at least when Johnny Cash played there.

Ex-LMS Class 4F 0-6-0, No.43924, pilots Ex-GWR 28xx Class 2-8-0, No.2807, across 'top field' - K&WVR.

More recently the group Banco de Gaia, (World Bank?), recorded Last Train to Lhasa, in support of those decrying Chinese involvement in Tibet – there is, now, a line linking China to Tibet. Despite the seemingly political nature of the track, and the line to Tibet, it uses some beautiful samples of steam locomotive sounds as it builds a – 'hypnotic rhythm' not unlike the hypnotic chants of the Tibetan Buddhist monks as they spin their prayer wheels. The relationship between railways and music isn't a one way street and just as modern musicians sample railway sounds the old railways would use musical terms as nick names for classes of locomotives – Gresley's K3 class 2-6-0s became known as Jazzers a reference to the similarity between the way the engines rode, (they swayed at the cab end) and the 'syncopated' exhaust beat of their three cylinders, which reminded the enginemen of the syncopated Jazz tunes and dance crazes that became popular in the years after WW I.

One of my own personal favourites is by the group Half Man Half Biscuit who do 'their' version of the theme tune from the Children's TV series Trumpton. In this song there's a line which contains the words 'time flies by when you're the driver of a train'. In a show designed for children, this line seems to imply a direct link between driving trains and enjoyment – time always 'flies by' when you are enjoying yourself. Strangely I don't ever remember children's TV shows with theme tune lyrics linking enjoyment with fat refining, slaughter men, or factory hands – time, it seems, does not fly by when you're stacking the shelves in Tesco. I know Benny Hill made us laugh with songs about milkmen and combine harvesters, and that Lonnie Donegan's dad was a dustman but, I cannot think of any other working class occupation which has such clear and unambiguous links to the enjoyment to be gained simply from doing the job as that of engine driving. There's another interesting link between railways, children's stories, and TV serials, one which has had far reaching consequences for the heritage railways themselves.

Ex-GWR 16xx Closs 0-6-0PT, No.1638, passing Bewdley South Signal Box, on the Severn Valley Railway.

In 1945 a clergyman called Awdry published the first, in what became a whole series, of books from the stories he had made up to amuse his young son. The nicely written and illustrated books were bought, in their thousands, as Christmas or Birthday presents for young boys – an interest in railways was, it seems, to be fostered from a very early age. During the early 1950s, the Rev. Awdry was a volunteer working on the first preserved railway in Britain, the narrow gauge Talyllyn Railway in Mid-Wales. Awdry's stories contained elements of events which had happened at, or on, the Talyllyn, unusually, for children's books, they also portrayed the railway in pretty much the way a real railway operates – though I'm not sure about using Jeremiah Jobling's bootlaces to effect running repairs to the brakes would happen too often. (From the story James and the bootlaces)

Over the years Awdry's stories proved to be very popular and, almost inevitably, they were picked up by television and made into a series for children. When the Rev. Awdry eventually retired from writing stories Awdry junior, (for whom the 'bed-time' stories had been created), took over the writing reins.  Keeping the stories true to the originals and including details from the national and preserved railway scene at the time of writing, Awdry Jnr. helped to keep the stories relevant to a new generation of kids – my own included. Former Beatles drummer Ringo Star was engaged to provide the narration and the series was filmed using model railway sets. In our 'hi-tech' world Jeremiah Jobling has a fan page on Facebook and his own Wikipedia entry – the steam age meets 21st century WWW.com.

Ex-LMS Class 3F 0-6-0, No.47406, with a freight for Rothley Brook, on the Great Central Railway.

The heritage railways themselves saw the possibilities in the Reverend Awdry's stories and began to put on events which had genuine 'family appeal'. Faces, more or less resembling those of the book illustrations, were hastily constructed and hung over the smoke box door of the most suitable Thomas, Percy, or James, lookalike, a corpulent member of the volunteers dressed as the Fat Controller patrolled the platform, recreating in full life size what had initially been no more than a bed-time story – albeit ones loosely based on the events of railway preservation. The 'Thomas' events have become so popular that they are now, along with the Santa Train / North Pole Express, one of the major revenue streams, for the heritage railways.

Ex-BR 2-6-4MTT No. 80105, piloting Ex-LNER Class D49 4-4-0, No.246 Morayshire, depart from Bo'ness with Santa's polar Express, on the Bo'ness & Kinneil Railway.

The gift shops stock all manner of Thomas products from Birthday cards and flags to books, CDs, models and jigsaws – all in all a nice little earner. Perhaps, the only fly in the ointment is that 'Thomas the Tank Engine' is, in this image conscious age, a 'franchise' and the railways have to pay fees/royalties to the Thomas franchise holders when they hold their Thomas events and the events have to meet standards laid down by the franchise holder. Probably the strangest connection I've come across, in relation to Thomas the Tank, comes from the German Bundesliga where the rather ample figure of the Bayer Leverkeusen manager has led to him being known as 'Herr Fat Controller'!! It would be a safe bet that the Reverend Awdry had no idea that his bed-time tales, for his young son, would spawn nicknames for German football team managers or, more importantly, become a major source of funding to one of the most ambitious pieces of industrial archaeology ever undertaken, which is what has happened.

There is little doubt that Thomas the Tank Engine has had an important, if not vital, role in the success of railway preservation but, there is an aspect of the whole Thomas phenomena that feeds directly into an area of preservation which has fared rather badly. In the Thomas stories the engines all have names, the coaching stock have names, even tractors and buses have names, we know the name of the 'authority figures' the Fat Controller, Sir Topham Hatt, and the Railway Inspector, Jeremiah Jobling, but there are, to all intents and purposes, no names for Thomas' driver and fireman - the footplatemen are anonymous. Very recently there has been a CGI production in which Thomas' driver is given a name, 'Bob', but there were no names in the original story, probably because 'you' were meant to imagine yourself in that role.  Despite the 'when I grow up I want to be an engine driver' ambition, held by many of the boys on the platform ends in the 1950s & 60s, the reality was, and is, very different - just like Thomas' driver the real world footplatemen, with a few very notable exceptions, were and remain anonymous.

Ex-Lancashire & Yorkshire Railway 0-6-0 No.957, and her crew, waiting for the 'right away' at Ingrow Station – K&WVR.

The Reverend Awdry isn't the only ecclesiastical connection in our ramble through the railway mindscape - rail and pulpit have a very long history, in fact they go all the way to the roots - to the first 'public railway' in the world – the Stockton and Darlington. Edward Pease, who was to become known as the Grandfather of Railways, his son

Joseph, the Backhouse family and a clutch of the other leading promoters of the Stockton & Darlington Railway were devout Quakers. (Darlington football club is nicknamed 'the Quakers' because of the town's historic links with Quakerism.) Quakers believed, and probably still do, that doing things for the benefit of everyone was an essential part of being a 'good Christian'. There is little doubt that doing things for the public good played a part in the decision making of these men. The extent to which they were intent on doing things for 'the public good' can, perhaps, be discerned from the Company Seal of the Stockton & Darlington Railway 'Periculum Privatum Utilitas Publica', which roughly translated is - 'at private risk for public service.'

Maybe we should think about that for a moment – a bunch of highly religious non-conformists put up their own money to provide something for public service. These men were merchants and bankers and there can be little doubt that they expected to return a profit from running the railway but the motto does suggest that profit was not the sole motivator.

Ex-GWR 94xx Class 0-6-0PT, No.9466, with the 'local' train to Quorn & Woodhouse – GCR.

Providing for the public good was all part of the purchase price of a ticket to heaven and the S&D would be that ticket. Over the centuries tickets to heaven have been purchased with all manner of currency; prayer, piety, self-sacrifice and, of course, the purchases of indulgences, (the sale of indulgences are credited with playing a role in the advent of the printing press), so why not buy a ticket to heaven by running a railway. Joking aside, the important piece of the motto – the 'for public service' is, I believe, the key to the essential difference between the way the railways began and what they became. The Stockton & Darlington railway wouldn't just make a profit for its owners it would allow those who used it to enhance and enrich their businesses too. The promoters of the Stockton and Darlington understood the 'utility' of what they were planning to provide and that it constituted a 'public good'. How many entrepreneurs today would put a motto like the S&D's on their company seal, let alone consider whether their enterprise provided any sort of 'public good'. The religious beliefs and sympathies of the Board of the Stockton & Darlington were not confined solely to the activities of the Stockton & Darlington and the other railways they built; they had, as we shall see later, far-reaching consequences for other railway speculators.

Darlington built, Ex-BR Class 2MT No.78019, pulling away from Hampton Loade Station – SVR.

Religious sentiment obviously played a part in the lives of other early railway pioneers, Timothy Hackworth, builder of the Rainhill trial entrant, 'Sans Pareil', was one such. Timothy Hackworth, who worked as 'Locomotive Superintendent' on the Stockton & Darlington from 1825 until 1840 was a devout Methodist and his refusal to work on the Sabbath, indirectly, cost him his job at Wylam colliery where, with William Hedley, he had been involved in the manufacture of the Wylam Dilly and Puffing Billy. Hackworth's role in the early development of the locomotive is often overlooked even though he is credited with the invention of the blastpipe and spring safety valves. His engine, Royal George, the first 0-6-0, built in 1827, for the S&D, was seen as an important improvement on those of Stephenson – it has even been suggested that it was Hackworth's engine the 'Royal George' which saved the day for steam traction on the 'Slow and Dirty'.

Hackworth, who had his own business and workshops in Shildon, also supplied the first steam locomotive for the St. Petersburg Railway and his son John Wesley Hackworth, (good Methodist names there), accompanied the engine on its perilous sea voyage to Russia; before helping to assemble the engine on arrival and train Russia's first footplatemen. There are suggestions that this included the Czar, a keen railway enthusiast, who had visited Britain some years earlier and was fascinated to see Murray & Blenkinsop's engines at work on Brandling's Colliery railway in Leeds. Staying in the North East, the Worsdell's were another devout Quaker family and, father and son both designed successful locomotives for the giant North Eastern Railway. It would not be hyperbole to state that the Quakers and other dissenting religious groups, Methodists, Baptists, Sandemanians and Glassites had, considering their overall numbers, a disproportionate influence on the whole of the industrial revolution, from iron and steel making, the Darby's of Coalbrookdale were Quakers, to banking, (the modern day Lloyds and Barclays are both the descendants of Quaker banks), railways, of course, and even electricity. (Faraday's religious beliefs, his family were Glassites, played a role in his subsequent understanding of the nature of electromagnetism.)

Ex-LNER Class D49 4-4-0, No.246 Morayshire, piloting Ex-LNER B1 Class 4-6-0 No.1306 Mayflower on the Llangollen Railway. No.246 Morayshire is carrying the Pre-1938 style Flying Scotsman headboard.

When the railways came to Scotland passenger trains did not run on Sundays for more than twenty years after their introduction elsewhere. So strong were the religious sentiments that in some areas when the Sunday trains were, eventually, put into service they were pelted with stones – well at least that bit is biblical. To put the religion into some sort of perspective there's a little tale from 2009 which shows how strong it can be. It was only in 2009 that, for the first time, there were ferry sailings from mainland Scotland to the Hebridean Islands on Sundays. The first boat to dock was met by a substantial group of the Islanders staging a silent protest, the same thing happened when Sunday air flights to the islands began.

If we move from the 'Wee Free' as the Free Church of Scotland is known, to religious sentiment with a more catholic twist we have this from the magazine Catholic Herald – '...there is a gravestone in Ely Cathedral bearing the inscription. 'The Spiritual Railway: The Line to heaven by Christ was made/ With heavenly truth the rails are laid, /From earth to heaven the Line extends./ To Life Eternal where it ends/ If you'll repent and turn from sin/ The train will stop and take you in.' If I were a gambling man I'd guess this poem was written by a devotee of the Great Western, God's Wonderful Railway to its fans, though why it should be on a tomb in Ely in the heart of Great Eastern territory is another matter. One church I myself have visited, in the village of Bolton – by – Bowland, has a stained glass window which depicts, of all things, a railway disaster. There is a more solid reminder of the railway's potential for death and destruction in the grave yard of a West Yorkshire church. During the construction of Bramhope tunnel on the Leeds to Harrogate route 24 navvies were killed in various accidents and floodings - a memorial to them, in the form of a scaled copy, in stone, of the north portal of Bramhope tunnel, was erected in Otley                                                        churchyard.

Ex-LNWR 0-6-2T, 'coal tank', No.1054, exits Mytholmes tunnel on the Keighley & Worth Valley Railway.

In the 1840s, when the line over Shap was being built, a more hands on approach was being taken by the church, as this extract from the time shows. 'The first doings of the workmen were anything but orderly, the neighbourhood for several miles around was filled with terror; shops were broken open, sheep slaughtered and cows milked!! Everything was frightfully lawless and disorderly, in one location near Shap there are about 500 men at work, and in a few weeks, the number will probably be doubled. The men have formed themselves into a colony on Shap fells where they have built for themselves their sod huts.

We rejoice to say, that active measures are on foot for their spiritual welfare, the railway directors have given every encouragement to the building of a church and schools, to which the Bishop of Carlisle gives his full sanction, and promise of lisense.[sic] A benevolent gentleman has contributed a large sum for the distribution of bibles; and the vicar of Crosby Ravensworth, through which parish the railway passes, is actively at work, circulating tracts, visiting the  families, attending the sick &c &c; and the kindly, grateful feeling which is induced, is most promising.' As told in the Christian Guardian (and Church of England magazine) of 1845, pages 68 & 69.

Ex-BR Class 4 2-6-4MTT, No.80002, banks Ex-LMS Class 2  2-6-2MTT, No. 41241, near Ingrow – K&WVR.

The almost ad hoc ministry provided to the navvies and their families, on Shap, in the 1840s had by the 1880s seen things move to a more organised institutional basis with the founding, in 1881, of the Railway Mission. This dedicated railway chaplaincy has been shepherding the railway flock ever since – truly men, and latterly women, on a mission. Saving souls and ministering to the needs of the sick and dying was, undoubtedly, a much more common occurrence on the railways of 1880s Britain than it is today. Some clergymen however, had very different relations with the operational railway and worked to save a very different kind of soul – the soul of the railway itself.

Two of the foremost railway photographers of the 20th century were clergymen, the Rev. A.W.V. Mace and the Reverend Eric Treacy, later Bishop of Wakefield. One of the Stanier Black 5s I fired on, during my spells at Farnley Jct., and Holbeck, was one saved from the cutter's torch, this engine, No.45428, is now preserved and operating on the North Yorkshire Moors Railway – it has been named 'Eric Treacy' not only to celebrate his photographic excellence but to honour the role he played in helping to keep open the former Midland Railway route now known, simply, as the 'Settle and Carlisle'.

Ex-LMS Princess Class 4-6-2, No.6201 Pricess Elizabeth, on the Settle – Carlisle line near Ais Gill.

 In the late 19th century the Reverend W.J. Scott a well-known locomotive performance recorder, (Gricer?), was one of the handful of men invited by the competing companies to time the trains involved in the Railway Races to the North in 1895. Peter Barham, a modern day railway enthusiast and the current incumbent of the parish of Ponteland, just north of Newcastle – upon – Tyne, regularly shows old railway films and documentaries in the church hall to raise money for charity. And, in similar vein, we cannot forget the late Rev. Teddy Boston who ran steam locomotives round his rectory garden at Cadeby and also had a substantial model railway layout which operated to a real timetable – if you're going to do it do it right!

For their part the railways were quite content to accept the services and ministry of the church though it must be said that, for many, this didn't extend so far as providing any financial assistance or services. Mammon might have been the deity of choice for the Directors, but the railways were quite happy to plunder the Biblical and the Saintly for the names of everything from their engine sheds to engines, and stations to signal boxes, even a locomotive building workshop was given the name of a Saint and in BR days there was an express service between Glasgow and Aberdeen which went by the name of Saint Mungo. During the Victorian era some railway companies even went so far as to coerce staff to attend religious services if they were not working on the Sabbath - 'on the Taff Vale Railway in 1856, religious observance was woven into the employees' lives by a rule which stated that the company 'earnestly requested that each of its servants 'on Sundays and holy days when he is not required on duty...will attend a place of worships; as it will be the means of promotion when vacancies occur.' (Taken from Turnip Rail web site.) Spiritual salvation and earthly promotion – or bribery and corruption, 'you pays your money and takes your choice'.

Ex-LMS Class 5 4-6-0 No.45428, now named Eric Treacy, with a demonstration freight working at Darnholme – NYMR.

Interesting as this detour down the God's End branch is we need to get back to the mainline, back on the road to the future. Railway architecture,  signalling equipment, rolling stock, not to mention bridges, viaducts and tunnels have all been saved from scrap or demolition and only a Philistine would consider this to be a bad thing. However, the almost miraculous saving of the 'hardware' of the railways has not been matched by, to anywhere near the same degree, the saving of the railway culture. Even the most important and frequently basic aspects of railway culture, the knowledge and skills associated with the safe operation of the railway do not have any recognised route for transmission from those with that knowledge to those people who now operate the heritage railways. This isn't a good thing, there are too many Chinese whispers, important considerations not clearly understood and I have lost count of the times I have watched trains being dragged, (brakes still rubbing and the regulator open), into the platform because the driver didn't know his braking points, applied too much brake, too soon, and then couldn't release them quickly enough. Basic train handling skill and route knowledge were the essentials a driver had to have, along with a very thorough knowledge of the Rule Book, before being allowed to take charge of his own train. Strange as this may seem to some, train handling and road knowledge were skills you learned over years not a few weekends. Firing over the same routes, again and again, moving engines around on shed, the occasional spot of 'driving' under supervision these were the things which taught you how to control your train, manage the fire and boiler, know where you were on the route.

Ex-LMS Class 5 4-6-0, No.44767, with a re-enactment of the Belfast Boat Express, which ran between Manchester and Heysham, leaves Loughborough through a halo of steam, smoke, and exhaust.

Lacking route knowledge and train handling skills is one thing, but there are other faults which need correcting which have nothing to do with route knowledge and everything to do with locomotive practice. I don't know if it is widespread, but at some lines it is a common fault, particularly at the North Yorkshire Moors Railway, Great Central Railway, and at the West Somerset Railway. I'm taking about setting off with the cylinder cocks open and leaving them open, not for one, or at most, two revolutions of the driving wheels, but for hundreds of yards at a time. This is not only poor practice it is potentially dangerous as; the driver cannot see the line ahead is clear of any obstructions, or if anyone is hand signalling, waving a flag, or hand lamp, to stop the train. In the case of the departure from Grosmont Station on the NYMR this is especially hazardous as drivers run into a tunnel with the taps, (cylinder drain cocks), open. On the fireman's side of the footplate there is a tendency to run around with the firehole doors wide open – not only is this not good practice it is also a contributor in the failure of tubes and stress cracking in the tube plate. People have been left badly burned through not having the firehole door properly closed, with the blower on, when entering a tunnel – again this is a lack of basic knowledge, both of good locomotive practice, and of the route.

The fireman, ensuring his fire irons are safely stowed befor departure, the locomotive is Ex-LB&SCR A1X Class 0-6-0 No.662.

On one occasion I remember watching as all manner of panic set in on the platform at Minehead. The train had arrived hauled by a Great Western Railway locomotive and was about to depart behind one from the former Great Eastern Railway. However, when the driver tried to start the train his engine slipped and snorted but moved barely a yard - after several failed attempts at getting started the head scratching began. What was wrong, the vacuum gauge in the cab showed that the brakes should be off, the hand brakes on the engine and in the guards van were off but, the train didn't want to budge. The answer was in the locomotives, Great Western engines create 25" of vacuum – thus even though the Great Eastern Railway engine had raised the required 21" of vacuum this hadn't been sufficient to fully release the brakes, which could only be done by someone going along the coaches 'pulling the strings' and thus releasing the brakes – again a lack of basic operating knowledge caused delay and confusion – until someone finally came along with the solution.

Ex-LNER Class A4 4-6-2,No.60007 Sir Nigel Gresley, with a set of teak coaches, at Darnholme – NYMR.

Clive Groome, who I've already mentioned, tried his very best to set up a worthwhile project to educate people, especially those who were involved, or were intending to become so, with the operation of steam locomotives on the preserved lines or national network. Clive's course was designed to pass on the practical skills and operating knowledge needed to safely handle a steam locomotive and its train, goods or passenger. The course involved learning about the routine tasks the driver performed on the locomotive, such as how to conduct a brake test, how to set for oiling, and tasks such as trimming and packing making before venturing onto the footplate, lighting up, raising steam, and preparing the engine to go off shed. There were explanations of the difference between the ejector and the injector, and the differences between live and exhaust steam injectors, just as there were of those between sight-feed and mechanical lubricators. Clive hoped, through this process of classroom study and practical hands-on work, to be able to pass on something of the engineman's culture as well as preparing volunteer footplate crews to safely operate the railway.

Clive's idea to retain the skills and knowledge base from hundred and fifty years of footplate working was taken up at many preserved railways, but not quite in the way he had imagined. Sadly, what happened was that Clive's carefully thought out and impeccably taught course of instruction degenerated into an arcade game – turn up, spend a few hundred pounds, and pretend to be an engine driver for the day. Not so much a course of necessary instruction in the skills and craft of the footplate but more of a fun day out, for those people lucky enough to have anything from £200 to £400 pounds pocket money to spend, playing in the cab of a steamer!!

Many of the old steam driven railway occupations simply disappeared and not even railway preservation could or should have saved them. However, even allowing for the fact that some jobs and skill sets simply disappeared the amount of effort and funding that has gone into preserving railway skills, craft, and culture – the 'software' of preservation – has been miniscule by comparison with the efforts of, and the sums raised for, 'hardware' projects. Preservation was never about saving anything other than the hardware, locomotives in particular, with engines being repatriated to this country from Finland, Sweden, South Africa and the USA, a by no means exhaustive list. In addition to repatriation there are numerous new build schemes and the new build A1 class 4-6-2 No. 60163 Tornado has already wowed the crowds and starred on Top Gear in a simulated Race to the North – echoing the events of 1888 and 1895 when the East Coast and West Coast routes did race each other between London and Aberdeen – front page headline events when they were taking place. Today, one simply cannot imagine 'racing trains' – 'elf 'n' safety mate, elf 'n' safety'.

Replica A1 Class 4-6-2, No.60163 Tornado, racing a horse, at Moorgates – NYMR.

On the 1960s steam driven railway you had to be 23 years old to be eligible to be passed-out for driver and over 16 to become a passed cleaner or fireman. Today, 2014, anyone with experience of mainline steam locomotive driving during the steam era is at least 70. The most junior of firemen at the end of steam would, today, be in his early 60s. For men with any length of service in these positions we are really talking about ex-firemen in their mid and late sixties and drivers aged 70 plus. Once these men have gone the knowledge, skills, and trade craft they had has gone with them - unless there is a great deal more emphasis put on preserving this aspect of our 'railway heritage'. I'm not talking about telling footplate tales but passing on the techniques involved and the knowledge gained from operating the railway on a day in day out routine. If the history of rail travel has taught us anything it is that 'if something can go wrong – it will'!

No.60163 Tornado, with the Scottish Railway Preservation Society's 'Fife Circle' Rail Tour, between Inverkeithing and North Queensferry, close to the Forth Bridge.

There is another reason for keeping alive these skills and preserving the knowledge and it is this. Thousands, possibly 10s of thousands, of men, women, and children died in creating the network of rails which bridged great rivers, tunnelled through the Pennines and under the Severn, spanned valleys and crossed Rannoch Moor. They built icons like the Forth Bridge and Ribblehead Viaduct and to this day we ride on a railway they built. They are the roots of our railways and as any gardener will tell you 'you've got to have roots in order to grow'. Where we came from is every bit as important as where we may be going and a failure to appreciate the mistakes of the past will simply lead to them being repeated in the future.

Even now, more than 45 years since steam ceased to provide the motive power for the railways, our common language is littered with railway oriented phrases - 'the wrong side of the tracks', 'running out of steam\puff', 'hitting the buffers'– no campaign or protest gets anywhere without first 'building up a head of steam'. The very word railway was itself made up or, should I say, eventually chosen from a number of competing terms, earliest among them was 'tram road' and 'wagon way' then there was railed way, sometimes railed-way both of which finally gave way to railway, but rail road, (a choice made by some other countries), was also in the running in the early days of 'the railway'.

Ex-(L)NER Q6 Class 0-8-0, No.63395, leaves Goathland sidings, as Ex-LNER A4 Class 4-6-2, No.60007 Sir Nigel Gresley, awaits the right away – NYMR.

Railwaymen too had their own language some of which would have alarmed those who didn't understand. 'Spent the last couple of hours knocking cripples out' isn't actually seriously reprehensible behaviour it is a term used by some footplatemen to describe certain forms of shunting - removing individual wagons with faults, defects, unlabelled, wrongly labelled, etc. from trains which had arrived at the goods yard, this also applied to coaching stock which was deemed unfit to run, for mechanical or other reasons. You could, 'put the bag in', you could, 'hit 'em up', or have 'a fitted head', you could, 'set back', 'ease up', or 'short rest' which translates, in order as; take water, in shunting set off very quickly then apply full brakes, (this sends one or more wagons trundling off into the chosen siding), several wagons behind the engine fitted with vacuum brakes giving a train more stopping power if most of the other wagons were 'unfittted', reverse into a siding, loop, etc. move the engine against the buffers of the coach or wagon to make coupling/uncoupling possible/easier, work a train to point B have three or four hours off-duty and then work the return to Point A.

Ex-GWR Manor Class 4-6-0, No.7828 Odney Manor, with a demonstration goods working, alongside Northwood Lane – SVR.

Such was the railway's relationship to daily life, everyday language, and the wider culture that it is, for all practical purposes, impossible to separate railway development from social and cultural change throughout the Victorian and Edwardian eras. Children's toys, supplies of fresh fruit, milk, fish, mail order household goods and trips to the seaside – the growth of suburbia, music, literature and the birth of the national daily newspaper, even the conduct of war, were all transformed or influenced by the railway and the steam locomotives which provided the driving force.

On the business front new companies began to appear; building locomotives, rolling stock, and signalling equipment for sale at home and abroad. UK Plc. was a major exporter of railway equipment, technology and even man power. British navvies were employed building lines in France, Canada, and the Crimea, in the case of the latter they are credited with actually helping turning the tide of battle and winning the campaign. In the French instance the British navvies were considered such a fearsome bunch that they were followed around the diggings and kept in order by the French army. The sale of British built locomotives, rolling stock, and signalling equipment helped both to advance the Empire and to ship its wealth back home to Britain. Strange though it may seem today, the earliest steam locomotives to run in America, in 1829, were built in Britain. The first was the 'Stourbridge Lion' one of four engines built by British Companies for the Delaware & Hudson Canal Co. Although the first engine to arrive in the USA was the Stephenson built, Pride of Newcastle, it was the Foster & Rastrick engine, Stourbridge Lion, which was used for the initial trials. In South America the Argentinian railways were largely funded by the British Empire, which is strange, given Argentina's more recent history with Britain.

Ex-LMS Class 5MT 2-6-0, No.42968, with a mixed goods working, near Loughboough – GCR.

Growing levels of share ownership and share dealing in railway company shares is credited with driving forward the creation of regional stock exchanges, such as those in Leeds, Liverpool and Manchester. 'Where there's muck there's brass' and foreign wars and conquests all have railway connections in their success. The late AJP Taylor, in one of his famous monologues on BBC television, tied the events leading up to general mobilisation in Germany at the commencement of the First World War to the planning which had been done on the German Railway timetable to make the mobilisation work, and that once it had begun stopping it was, according to Taylor, for all practical purposes, impossible. During the same war we shipped the locomotives of, amongst others, the North British and Great Western Railway to the battle fields of France. When these engines 'came home from the war' some of the North British contingent were given the names of Generals, and those of the sites of battles, – quite an honour as the North British Railway were not in the habit of anything quite so frivolous as bestowing names on 0-6-0 goods engines. However, in keeping with spirit of prudence which characterises much that is North British the names were only 'painted on' – no fancy copper and brass here!

Ex-GWR Hall Class 4-6-0, No.4936 Kinlet Hall, alongside Northwood Lane – SVR.

If winning wars, securing the Empire, making 'loadsa' money and changing the Nation's eating, drinking and socialising  wasn't enough the  railways even provided the seed bed for some of the earliest uses of electrical power, in improving safety and speeding up the passage of trains. So far this is all so upbeat, but there is, as ever, with matters railway, a downside.

There were plenty of shareholders who lost their shirts on hare-brained schemes, crackpot ideas, and, it must be said, to scams and skulduggery, even their graces the Bishops of Durham were not above making a fast buck out of land deals with railway promoters. The number of individuals  'trashing' their inheritances or 'pulling a scam' were dwarfed by the numbers of railway employees who lost their lives because of unsafe working practices, excessive hours at work and the mechanical or other failures of the emergent technology. From the beginning of the railway age to the start of the 20th century the loss of life and serious injuries amongst railway employees was horrendous 500 + deaths a year, (that's more every year than the number of soldiers killed during the 10 years we've been bringing democracy to Afghanistan), and more than 68,000 serious injuries a year, are the sort of numbers we're talking about.

Those who would defend the railway companies usually resort to saying that; 'deaths from poor working conditions and practices were a feature of a great many Victorian businesses from mining to textiles', as though this in some way mitigated the circumstances. Perhaps, more pertinent is the fact that the railways treated their passengers only marginally better than their workforce – often only employing the most up to date safety systems, like effective brakes for example, when Parliament obliged them to do so. This usually followed some particularly gruesome accident involving much loss of life and, possibly more importantly, serious damage to property.

Ex-GCR Class 04 2-8-0, No.63601, a member of the National Collection, approaching Quorn & Woodhouse – GCR.

In 1887 there was a particularly nasty accident at Hexthorpe, (near Doncaster), on what was then the Manchester Sheffield & Lincoln Railway, as was the custom at that time, the driver and fireman were put on trial for manslaughter. However, unlike in all previous cases this time the footplatemen had professional representation in court and the services of expert witnesses - hired by their union. ASLEF had been founded seven years earlier in 1880 and by 1887 had accrued sufficient members and funds to be able provide their members with legal services. The crew involved in the Hexthorpe crash were acquitted and, to this day, footplatemen still join ASLEF for the legal representation provided, for all members. There is little doubt that in terms of railway history and that of those railway workers most often lionised by enthusiast and public alike, (the footplatemen), the Hexthorpe crash was a truly significant watershed. It is this crash that is commemorated in the stained glass of the church in Bolton – by –Bowland. The window was paid for by the widower of one of the victims of the crash.

Passing freights, Ex-LMS 8F 2-8-0, No.48476, (48305), with a train of mineral empties passes Black 5, No.45231 Sherwood Forester, travelling north with a mixed goods, at Quorn & Woodhouse – GCR.

The real cause of the Hexthorpe crash was the suspension, by the MS&LR, of block working. The 'block' had been suspended because it was race day at Doncaster and more trains could be moved and more money made if the safety of the travelling public was compromised. (A block section is, very crudely speaking; the gap between one signal boxes' last starting signal and the home signal of the next signal box. In normal block working no train would be allowed to enter this section until the proceeding train had cleared the advanced starting signal of the box ahead.) Despite the acquittal of the footplate crew no charges were brought against the MS&LR even though there could be little doubt that they were culpable. A secondary or contributing factor in the crash was the type of braking system then in use on the MS&LR - a form of vacuum brake which had already been shown to have serious defects and whose use was subsequently outlawed, in 1889, by an act of parliament. It is also worth remembering that although many passengers and railway employees have, over the years, lost their lives, and many more have been injured there have not been any prosecutions of railway management or owners – though many innocent railwaymen did go to jail, blamed for accidents they couldn't have prevented – scapegoats for their unscrupulous employers.

Under these circumstances one might expect that a work on railway accidents, which is thought by many to be authoritative, and especially one that has been reprinted no less than six times over a period of 40 years, would contain some of the details mentioned above - it does not. The coverage afforded by the Talyllyn's saviour, Tom Rolt, in 'Red for Danger', of this highly significant incident, is a travesty.

'The driver of an express from Manchester to Hull overran signals and crashed into the rear of a race special which was standing at Hexthorpe ticket platform, killing twenty - five people. This accident was remarkable for the fact that the all the employees of the company offered to forgo a day's wages in order to defray the costs of the disaster.' ("Red for Danger" Rolt, T.)

Ex-GWR Manor Class 4-6-0, No.7802 Bradley Manor, between Winchcombe and Toddington – GWSR.

The really 'remarkable' fact about the Hexthorpe crash entry in Red for Danger is that it neglects to mention ASLEF's provision, for the first time ever, of legal representation for the footplate crew and it fails to explain that the 'foregoing' of a day's wages was not exactly a spontaneous gesture but one decided upon by a lickspittle junior management in which the rest were obliged to acquiesce. Though, to be fair, the company did say thank you and refused the offer. Making matters worse 'Red for Danger' fails to make clear the reason why the driver over-ran signals and that the footplate crew were exonerated, thus leaving the reader with the totally false impression that the crew were at fault.

Regular reprinting of 'Red for Danger', has had the potential to ensure that a large number of individuals, whose interest in matters railway extends to the printed word, may come to hold views about the activity of the railway companies which might reasonably be described by the word benign. Rolt's partiality in favour of the companies is not an isolated case, there is almost a tradition within certain areas of railway historiography to portray the companies and the individuals who ran and managed them in a highly selective manner, often romantising their activities and painting their owners, managers, and chief engineers as heroic individuals.

If the propensity for heroic tosh was confined to 'poor' railway history books, it might not be so bad; but when he was the Tory Education minister Michael Gove and former Tory minister, and self-styled railway aficionado,

Michael Portillo want(ed) to see history of this type back on the curriculum – ah! Michael Portillo, speaking at the 1995 Tory party conference said he wanted to see; "a return to a history of heroes, not the sociological flim-flam that passes for history". Yes, that's what they want, history written by the victors, no ifs, no buts, this is propaganda pure and simple. The tragic part is that vast numbers of people buy into this nonsense believing that somehow this is 'proper' history. The problem with Portillo and Gove's view is that the sociological flim-flam is a far better interpretation and explanation of what has gone before than any historical account based simply on the actions and activities of so called 'heroic individuals'.

Ex-GWR 45xx Class 2-6-2T, No.5526, with an Auto-train service on the Llangollen Railway.

There is, of course, the ever present possibility of using heroic portrayals of the past to 'create' politically useful 'myths',  of a type which Messrs Gove & Portillo would wholly endorse. The creation of such heroic and mythologised histories may subsequently be used to justify present or future modes of political activity across a broad spectrum of social and cultural institutions - much as Orwell's dictum describes - "He who controls the past, controls the future, he who controls the present controls the past", ( Orwell, "1984" ). The twin assaults on history, on its constituents, and on how it should be publicly communicated are important considerations in how the nation understands its past.

Ex-SR Battle of Britain Class 4-6-2, No.34053 Sir Keith Park, at the summit of Eardington Bank – SVR.

The real difficulty with delving into aspects of railway history that do not fit the parameters of the 'heroic' and 'rose tinted' representations which are such a predominant narrative in much that passes for railway history in books, on the heritage railways, and in railway museums is that they first have to attack these prejudices before they themselves can be heard. Some years ago I provided an article, for the magazine Steam World, on the railways during WWII titled 'Mainline Front line'. This article debunked some of the myths of a nation all pulling together in the 'Dunkirk spirit' by looking at what was happening between the railway companies and their employees during the war years. The ensuing post bag was so large it had to be carried over two subsequent issues and some of the correspondents were practically incandescent with outrage – they were, in a word, steaming! Such was the level of intolerance of the idea of free speech that several of the letters explicitly stated that if the magazine published this sort of thing again they would cease to buy it.

Anything which threatens widely held beliefs, even if they are just that – belief, rather than a set of cogent explanations for the available evidence, is immediately attacked and vilified. In many cases when opposing widely held beliefs with a series of evidence based information which attack and undermine these beliefs the attack is simply dismissed, and marginalised, making alternative accounts of the nature of reality even harder to disseminate. Some Gricers will view undermining Rolt's 'Red for Danger' as an act of treachery made worse by the fact that it also maligns the companies who owned and ran the railways. For a great many the real reality of preservation is that it presents only the rose tinted view and, more importantly, they would not have it any other way. The journey back in time on preserved railways, or in railway museums, and in much of the literature is a 'time capsule' from which connections to factual or unpleasant correspondences have been expunged. In order to keep the capsule 'time tight' anything which threatens the myths which support it have to be attacked to keep the time seal 'tight'.

Ex-BR Class 5 4-6-0, No.73129, pilots Ex-BR Class 8P 4-6-2, No.71000 Duke of Gloucester, across Summerseats viaduct on the East Lancashire Railway.

Doubtless there will be Gricers who see this book as sacrilege and some of the people who have spent half a lifetime as volunteers, rebuilding, running, and maintaining the preserved railways will probably feel betrayed. However, this would be to miss the point and contradict the fact that what has actually been done represents 'an heroic achievement' not by some 'heroic' individual but by tens of thousands of people working together with a common purpose. This railway commune(ity)  is as important an achievement as the saving of the railway hardware and if preserved railways are to have a future it is this community which must be sustained. The railway they seek to preserve and maintain ended in 1968 and unless there's some weird catastrophe in which the nation is suddenly transported back to 1948 it has gone. Even the regular services of steam rail tours on the national network, such as the Jacobite or the Cumbrian Mountain Express cannot begin to replicate the everyday railway of the 1950s.

Ex-LMS Princess Royal Class 4-6-2, No.6201 Princess Elizabeth, heading the 'up' Cumbrian Mountain Express, near Cumwhinton, at the start of the S&C.

'Red for Danger', seems to feed people's desire to rubber-neck as much as it does to discover the implications and findings of Railways Inspectorate Accident Reports, particularly as these reports are dull fare indeed when compared with the drama of tales from the footplate; of bacon and eggs fried on the shovel, of dashing down the mainline or slogging over the Cumbrian fells up mile after mile of 1 in 75. Similarly the tedious detail involved in uncovering and explaining financial wrong doing is never going to quicken the pulse. When it comes to dealing with the fact that substantial sums of money, genteelly referred to as 'West Indian Funds', a euphemism for 'money made from the buying and selling of slaves', were involved in railway construction it is quite definitely a case of the less said the better.

Then as now the gutter press were not above running a good scare story and even a good scam wasn't hard to find. Today we have 'whiplash' injury claims from road traffic accidents - back in the 1890s they had 'railway spine' – supposedly caused by the jolting of the carriages. Today we have metal thieves stealing cabling etc. from our railway network, then we had metal thieves stealing locomotive parts, up to and including an entire boiler, from outside railway workshops in Miles Platting (Manchester). Higher up the greasy pole, today, we have corporate greed and bankers' bonuses, then they had 'insider trading' and banking collapses, (Overend & Gurney in a scandal involving the London Chatham & Dover and North British Railways), only the names have changed and none of them are innocents.

Our glorious railways have closets full of little but skeletons, and, for a great many, the view is that is where they should remain – in the closet. The Gravy Train, a piece of American railroad slang which entered common parlance during the 1920s, is pretty much synonymous with railway company practices from the earliest days of the railway age and, what is more, it is still going on as I write. The railways have simply transported vast sums of the public's money into the pockets of already very, very, wealthy individuals. For the money that has been supposedly spent on 'improving' our 'railway experience' we should be riding in coaches trimmed with Ermine, on tracks made from gold, laid on a ballast of diamonds – dream on.

Ex-GWR 0-6-0PT, No.6435, passing Bewdley South Signal Box, on the Severn Valley Railway.

One of the more recent examples of railway chicanery even gave a nod to 'our railway heritage' in more ways than one. Back in the 'days of olde', the route from London to Edinburgh and Aberdeen was operated by numerous companies who both co-operated and competed, some of them were large undertakings like the Great Northern Railway, others, like the Great North of England Railway, were much smaller. The Great North of England Railway was absorbed into the giant North Eastern Railway long before the Amalgamation which created the London &

North Eastern Railway in 1923. Small it might have been but the Great North of England Railway has its own rather special little entry in the railway hall of shame.

Seventy years after the Amalgamation took place and more than 40 years after railway Nationalisation the government of the day, in 1993, decided to sell-off the Nationalised Railways but there was a problem – how do you sell something which is, to your average comedian, the stock in trade of his comic repertoire. From curled up sandwiches to the wrong kind of snow, from stuck in a siding to dilapidated rolling stock - the railway was a laughing stock. With the practiced legerdemain of a well versed con-man the Admen hitched their wagons to the 'heritage' railway. People went to the 'heritage' railways for enjoyment and to wallow in the rose tinted past and the 'privatised' railway would revive those halcyon days. Everything was going to be chocolate and cream, warm beer, cricket on the village green - an 'Olde Ingerland' that never existed.

Ex-SR Class S15 4-6-0, No.825, departing from Grosmont Station – NYMR.

The new sales appeal of the rebranded railway was to be based on nostalgic images of our 'railway heritage' as it said on the freshly repainted coaches on the East Coast Mainline 'the route of the Flying Scotsman'. The 'new olde image' was trailed and trumpeted at every possible level in every conceivable way. John Major, then, Prime Minister wittered on in newspapers and on the TV about warm beer and the GWR. Mr Dow, at the time The Keeper of the NRM, appeared on Calendar, the YTV evening news programme, telling all who'd listen that they enjoyed a better service from York to London than they did in 1935 and in these and a myriad of other ways one and all was led to believe that it all heralded a 'great' railway revival.

Ex-LNER A4 Class 4-6-2, No.60009 Union of South Africa, near Wormit, shortly after crossing the Tay.

The rebranding and appeals to nostalgia were not confined to the initial process of selling-off, (giving away?), the national network, some of the newly formed companies chose to plunder the heritage lockers of their particular bits of the former nationalised network in order to create the kind of public image they wanted to present. One of these companies, Sea Containers Ltd., was under the command of Mr James Sherwood who had more than a passing interest in steam preservation, being, at the time, the owner of the V.S.O.E. franchise.

By now some of you will probably have worked out what the connections are between Great North of England Railway, shares, and railway heritage. For those of you who haven't here are some more clues, this time provided by the man once charged with running the passenger services between Kings Cross and a great many points north, Christopher Garnett CEO of GNER. 'The most visible change is of course the new name - Great North Eastern Railway ... Inevitably this will be shortened to the initials GNER, and I expect (and hope) that this acronym will be as well-known and respected as the LNER was some 50 years ago... New names and new colour schemes make the most obvious statements about moving away from the British Rail past'. To paraphrase a well know phrase from George Orwell's Animal Farm, in selling the railways it was to be, 'BR bad L.N.E.R. good'

Ex-LNER Clas J72 0-6-0, No. 69023, alongside Northwood Lane on the Severn Valley Railway.

When Garnett made these remarks GNER had invested considerable amounts of time and money, reportedly £2 million, with two branding / design consultancies neither of whom appear to have noticed that the route whose virtues they were extolling already had connections to the acronym GNER - despite all the rhetoric about the knowledge of the 'glorious past' of the companies involved. In seeking to create a heritage that GNER 1996 could improve upon, the image consultants chose a name which generated as initials those of a company which once owned part of the very route that was being 'rebranded'.

In their earnest desire to create, for their paymasters, the right kind of brand image the intrepid consultants appear to have completely overlooked the old GNER or to give it its full title the Great North of England Railway. It is, perhaps, quite fitting that this particular acronym should have been the choice of a company (Sea Containers Ltd.) involved in one of the most scandalous give-aways in history - for it was the old GNER's claim to shame to have been the company involved in the unscrupulous share dealings which, in the 1840s, brought down the 'Railway King', George Hudson, himself.

The original GNER was one of those railways built and owned by the Stockton & Darlington and their religious beliefs were at odds with the business practices of Hudson, who was desperate to control the GNER to establish control over the entire route from Kings Cross to Edinburgh. In his desperation to gain control Hudson began acquiring shares illegally and two stock exchange employees Messrs Love and Dance discovered his dirty dealings and the plot was up. Shady share dealings, a Government desperate to 'privatise' at any cost and - and thus history repeats itself today as farce.

Ex-GNR N2 Class 0-6-2T, No1744, sets off from Oakworth Station – K&WVR.

There are several possible explanations as to why Sea Containers Ltd. might have chosen a name which can be linked to one of the more sordid episodes of 'railway heritage'. One possibility is that someone didn't do their homework and they did not know about the Great North of England Railway (GNER) and the share dealing scandal surrounding it. Another explanation might be that they did know about these connections and chose to ignore them, perhaps, in the belief, in my view correctly, that so few people would know about the old GNER that it simply didn't matter - no one would notice and if they did - well they were likely to be a bunch of 'puffer nutters' so it didn't matter anyway. Whatever the reasons behind Sea Containers' choice of GNER there is little doubt that the choice was based on the use of 'railway heritage' as a sales aid - that is 'railway heritage' is simply being used as a tool in a fairly cynical attempt to manipulate public perception.

In their own ways the examples afforded by the Hexthorpe incident and its coverage in 'Red for Danger', and the selection of a new name for the East Coast route operator, illustrates the difficulties of dealing with our railway heritage as though it were a commodity. In the second example corporate ignorance or arrogance, probably both, reshapes the past to suit its own perceptions about the future, to add value, status, even gravitas to its undertakings. However, the first example is, perhaps, more insidious for, in this case, the plea of ignorance is unavailable. In 'Red for Danger's' case an insider, and 'authority' is being selective, editing out details of the events which do not suit his world view. In reading 'Red for Danger' you would have no inkling that the Hexthorpe crash provided a turning point in industrial relations on Britain's Railways – or that it set a precedent which is still, more than 120 years later, a vital aspect of all rail crash investigations - the legal representation of the crew. In fact you may well gain the impression that the crew were guilty despite their exoneration - history of this sort is just another commodity, which for some people is to be used to earn a living or create a past more in tune with their own prejudice. We should take great care to ensure these forms of misuse do not cover up and confuse the real nature of the process called history.

Hunslet 0-6-0ST, No.3839 Wimblebury, exits Dilhorne Colliery sidings, on the Foxfield Railway.

Leaving behind the hubris of 'big business' engine and crew go 'off shed' and head for the station to collect their train and begin the journey. Flags, whistles, and most importantly signals, are waved, blown, and set, respectively. Are you sitting comfortably? Then we'll begin. It might seem obvious today that some form of control over such basic things as which direction along the line a train would travel was an essential – not in the beginning it wasn't. On the Stockton & Darlington trains were hauled by locomotives, by horses, and by rope and stationary engines.

Let's just say that disputes of all kinds broke out, some ended badly, and others ended/started in the pub, as these gems from C.A.McDougall's The Stockton & Darlington Railway 1821 – 1861 neatly illustrate.

'Two horse-leaders who left Shildon in a drunken condition on 1st March, 1832, met the "William IV" ascending an incline. They refused to take to the siding, blocked the line with a rail and chair and finally mounted the engine and assaulted the driver.' 'On the 4th August, 1831, a number of horse drawn empty wagons left Stockton and a driver got into the dandy-cart in front of his wagon and fell asleep. His leaderless horse dropped behind and eventually came to a stop. The "Globe" coming up behind ran into the standing wagons and threw them off the line.' McDougall doesn't tell us what happened to the sleeping driver – it would certainly have been a 'rude awakening'.

Ex-BR Class 4 2-6-0, No.76079, rumbles through Goathland with a demonstration goods train – NYMR.

Obviously this, 'it's your round', free-for-all situation couldn't be allowed to continue and some basic operating rules began to emerge. Growing numbers of lines created new operational difficulties and requirements – some of which bordered on farce. (Trains from Aberdeen to Inverness, for example, were deliberately sent off from Aberdeen at times which ensured that passengers for stations to Inverness travelling from Edinburgh, Glasgow or London would miss them. I doubt that Aberdeen hoteliers complained too much about this particular practice.)

Stage left: enter a man with the red flag, closely followed by Michael Faraday. The opening of the Liverpool & Manchester might have heralded the arrival of what was to become a public railway network but without Faraday's discovery of electricity, and the many experiments which followed, it might never have got off the ground. Pootling along behind a man with a red flag, or being sent off on time intervals with no knowledge of what lie ahead – particularly where lines were on a bend through cuttings, or went through tunnels, was never going to work. Electricity would provide the solution, as it has for so many things – but what strange stuff it is. You make it by spinning coils of copper wire round a magnet and it can be used to kill you or bring you back to life. You cannot see it, or smell it, it doesn't leak out of the plug sockets and it has so transformed the world we live in that it is almost impossible to conceive of a life without it.

Ex-LB&SCR A1X Class 0-6-0, No.662, stands outside Toddington Signal Box, on the Gloucestershire Warwickshire Steam Railway.

Before the miracle of the electric telegraph, (Cooke & Wheatstone 1838), the railway policeman with his trusty watch told the driver when he could set off – and there is a direct connection between him and his modern day counterpart the signaller – the slang term for a policeman 'Bobby'. To generations of railwaymen the signalman was always 'Bobby' and they are still known thus today. Back in ye olde days it would be the fireman's duty to go to the signal box if his train was brought to a stand by signals for any length of time – immediately during fog or snow.  Behind all this stands Rule 55 – 'Detention of trains on running lines' – it has many sub-clauses and all would have to be known by heart before being 'passed' for firing duties. Rule 55 was the Ten Commandments and it occupies 10 pages in the British Railways Rule Book 1950 Ed.  One of the ways a young footplateman learned chunks of the rule book was through the use of little rhymes and mnemonics. Part of one of those rhymes related to me to help memorise rule 55 was; 'during fog and falling snow/ to the box o' you must go'. The mnemonic for the constituents of coal was 'No Cash' – Nitrogen, Oxygen, Carbon, Ash, Sulphur, and Hydrogen – railwaymen never had any cash so it was a piece of cake to remember.

Once at the signal box and having carried out his duties the fireman would trudge back to the engine, having ensured that before he left the signal box the signalman had put a collar on the signal protecting his train. (The collar prevented the signalman from pulling the lever allowing a train to enter the section behind the train.) From my own railway career I remember, when on freight workings, with some of the more remote signal boxes you could be stopped at the home board and then waved up to the box where the Bobby would ask for a few shovels full of coal for his stove. I have even read of trains being operated outwith the working timetable to provide, coal and water to shunter's cabins, signal boxes and other out-posts in large marshalling yards. These ad hoc services were often operated directly by the men themselves with junior management turning a blind eye to the activities.

Ex-GWR 14xx Class 0-4-2T, No.1450, on an Auto-train working, passes Bewdley South Signal Box – SVR.

Despite the difficulties, both technical and operational, new lines grew and signals proliferated but not all the signs were good. Some signals went up, some went down, and some even somersaulted. There were rotating discs and arms, hand signals, fog signals, shunting signals, red lights, white lights, engine whistle signals, block bell signals, all that was missing was 'old uncle Tom Cobleigh'. There were even signals which allowed you to pass other signals set at danger - on the railway there's always an exception, not all of them Sundays only. This plethora of conflicting signalling arrangements is just one of the less well documented side effects of Victorian laissez faire capitalism at work on the railway. That such a level of signalling confusion led to accidents comes as no surprise - indeed what is surprising is that it didn't create many more.

Confusing signals can lead to catastrophic results – not all signals are your signals. (Taking the wrong signal is exactly what happened in the dreadful crash, at Ladbroke Grove, in October 1999, the driver took the wrong signal and two trains collided with disastrous consequences.) Signals signal changes of direction, or permission to move forwards or back, turn left, turn right, no best not turn right that only leads to trouble. I'm getting confused now, which way am I going, forwards or back? Well, now, that depends on which way you were facing to begin with. London was always the Up, you went to Scotland on the Down but everyone knows Scotland is north of London and it's 'allus oop north'! The North, generally supposed to begin somewhere beyond Bedford, was 'industrial', 'foggy', riddled with mills if not actually plagued with boils. Respectable people only went there to inspect what generated the vastness of their wealth; the mines, and factories churning out cotton or wool and no shortage of flannel.

Ex-SR N15, 'King Arthur', Class 4-6-0, No.30777 Sir Lamiel, at Castlehill, on the West Somerset Railway.

Railways, like Tulips before them, became a mania for the Nouveau Riche – everyone wanted one to come to their town, to put them on the railway map, well nearly everyone - NIMBYism isn't a new phenomenon. Lords and Ladies, Squires and assorted members of the 'Landed Gentry' made the railways go round or under their land – they even had them build fanciful parapets, portals, or mock castellation to hide their hideous new 'railway age' creations. One line, in Manchester, was cut through a pauper's graveyard, the navvies dug up the bodies, some buried in graves up to 9 bodies deep, some in wooden boxes, others not. Not all the skeletons in the railway's locker were euphemisms. There are no architectural disguises here and the navvies well, they just swilled their beer, ate the beef, and carried on digging. Not a job for the faint-hearted, building the country's railways. There are no surprises here, no contradictions between church on Sunday, exploit thy neighbour on Monday and every other day too. This is the trackbed the railway was built on, not stone ballast, iron rail, and wooden sleepers, but on dead navvies, their wives and their children, dead paupers, uprooted from their final rest and all under the baleful glare of the god fearing, church going, hypocrites, preying through the eye of a needle, as they got richer in the process. There are some signals it's impossible to miss.

Ex-BR Class 4 2-6-4T, No.80002, pilots Ex-BR Class 5 4-6-0, No 73129, out of Damems loop – K&WVR.

Down the ages, 'we don't want to send out the wrong kind of signals', is a constant mantra from governments of every hue and political persuasion. With this in mind we might well ask what kind of signals do the heritage railways send out. It might also be fair to ask if these messages are the result of some carefully thought out strategy or merely the by-product of everyday heritage railway operations and the landscapes and mindscapes within which they take place.

War Export 8F, 2-8-0, Turkish State Railways No.45160, rolls through Quorn & Woodhouse Station, GCR.

One thing I've noticed, in visiting heritage railways, all round the country, for more than 30 years, is that despite the huge numbers of people who do enjoy a day out at a heritage railway members of the Black and Asian communities are practically invisible – could this be that for them the 'signals' don't point the way to summers past spent on the platform end, of journeys to the seaside or off to boarding school, but rather to days spent cleaning toilets, clearing tables and washing up in the station buffet, or sweeping platforms and cleaning carriages on breadline wages - I doubt that heritage railways seem quite so nostalgic if these are your railway memories. It might be an interesting exercise to run a 'Last Train to Skaville' event – a sort of Notting Hill Carnival of Steam. One thing is certain it would be a more colourful event than 'Wartime Weekend'. Quite how heritage railways became part of a re-enactment of an exceedingly mythical WWII I'm not sure and more especially as the railwaymen were treated very shabbily during the war. (Most heritage railway fans weren't even born when WWII was raging across Europe and the Far East.)

In the public's, 'nostalgic' consciousness the war is associated with 'the Dunkirk spirit', 'pulling together' - views difficult to reconcile with many of the letters and columns in the Locomotive Journal, as these exchanges on the cost and availability of food rations for footplatemen demonstrate: 'One of the most urgent matters... is that of making adequate and effective arrangements for providing those of our men called upon to work long hours... with... extra food... The simple fact is that in West-End restaurants... food, etc., can be obtained almost without practical limit, whilst the needs of vital war workers are too little attended to.... Lord Woolton, a successful businessman... and Minister of Food doing his job of ensuring fair distribution on the basis of need he has been anything but a success.... he is reported to have said about rationing: 'It is not my job to achieve social equality.' (Collick, P.; Locomotive Journal; 1941, 168) (Driver Percy Collick was Assistant General Secretary of ASLEF and was later elected an M.P. & his column Parliamentary Jottings became a regular feature in the Journal)

Ex-LMS Class 4MT 2-6-4T, No.42085, with the TPO, shortly after leaving Loughborough – GCR.

It would seem, however, that 'social equality' did not even extend as far from the footplate as the station buffet. These letters from a driver at Gorton, (Manchester) and another from Rugby are typical on this aspect of a nation 'pulling together'. The Gorton driver wrote to the Journal expressing his appreciation of the Y.M.C.A. in general and the branches at Sheffield and Nottingham in particular for their help in providing sustenance to men, like himself, stuck many miles from home waiting for their return workings. However, his letter continues: 'One regrets the same cannot be said of the refreshment room staff at that station, [Sheffield Victoria], where snobbery seems the order of the day and Loco men anathema.' (Locomotive Journal; 1941, 246)

The Rugby driver picks up the theme: 'In the L.M.S. refreshment rooms at Rugby we get nothing but black looks... For myself and, I dare say other loco men, we have nothing to thank these places for, although we are all supposed to be working for the same cause (Win the War).' (Locomotive Journal; 1941, 286)  The Rugby driver's letter isn't the most scandalous of the letters to the Journal on this issue;  as driver Carter of Willesden makes the following comments: 'As the L.M.S.R. have not found a solution to relieve their train crews in eight hours, but allow men to work between ten and twenty-four hours for a day's work, they have introduced a food scheme for emergency, called "Iron Rations." This 'wonderful service' entitles a man to a teaspoonful of tea and a teaspoonful of sugar for a penny.   As 1lb of tea contains 144 teaspoonful's, the company makes an amazing profit of 300% on tea and 1340% on sugar at present day prices.' (J.A.Carter Willesden L.D.C Jan. 1941)

Ex-GWR 45xx Class 2-6-2T, No.4566, at Farm Crossing, Northwood Lane, near Bewdley – SVR.

Looking back on wartime events without the nostalgia goggles created by countless showings of Reach for the Sky, Brief Encounter, or documentaries on Vera Lynn, a harsher less romantic picture emerges. Dunkirk had been and gone, but the mainline remained the frontline and naturally enough examples of bravery are not hard to find. Men like driver I.T. Davies and fireman F.R.Newns of Birkenhead who were awarded the George Medal for their life saving actions during an air raid in 1940. Davies and Newns were, undoubtedly, heroic and their medals well deserved, but the pages of the Journal illustrate a more down to earth, common or garden, element of bravery like this report from driver J.V.Sweeney Organising Secretary of No.6 District: 'It is not possible to compile a few notes ...without writing about some of the effects of the bombing... most of our time now being taken up with visiting members who have suffered the loss of their homes and all their belongings,... at a recent meeting of the London District Council [none] will forget the arrival of the secretary ...and his simple statement. 'I cannot stay with you my house was bombed to the ground in the night.' (Locomotive Journal; 1941, 214)

Ex-SR Battle of Britain Class 4-6-2, No.34070 Manston, exits Loughborough Station – GCR.

Sweeney continues his report with a harrowing account of the actions of two other footplatemen who went to the aid of their wounded and dying colleagues on one of the London termini during an air raid. 'Within three minutes of attaching, a bomb fell close to their engine killing the driver and severely wounding the fireman. The driver and fireman at the stop block end of the train immediately rushed to the spot, and using a platform trolley lifted the bombed men from the footplate ...proceeding along the platform road a few yards a second bomb crashed in the vicinity.... within a few seconds a third bomb fell a few yards away. Blinded by dust and smoke, ... they struggled through... handed over their charge to a First Aid squadron. (Locomotive Journal; 1941, 214)

Throughout the war the issues such as pensions, wage rises to off-set war induced inflation, discipline, and injury compensation were serious considerations for working footplatemen and in his review of the society's achievements during 1940, the General Secretary raised the issue of compensation for injuries sustained as a result of working during enemy action: 'The closing months of the year began to bring to light the effect of the intensified enemy action on this country. The railways, as a legitimate point of attack, naturally were not left free from enemy raiders, and therefore casualties resulted... The policy of the Government seeking the co-operation of all concerned in the national war effort in working after the siren, brought this position vividly before everybody. Whilst not objecting to the principle we set out to get an undertaking from the Companies, that should any man meet with injury through working until danger was imminent, that he would not be treated less favourably than he would be had he a claim under the Workmen's Compensation Act. The Companies declined to accept this liability on the grounds that it was a matter for a national decision.' (Locomotive Journal; 1941, 5)

Ex-BR Class 9F 2-10-0, No.92214, on a fitted goods, passes a crop of Gricers, near Loughborough – GCR.

Rank and File opinion on this issue, at the time, can best be summed up by the Resolution passed by King's Cross branch: '...nothing less than full wages in such circumstances will meet the approval of our members. (Locomotive Journal; 1941, 67) The reality faced by injured footplatemen was a far cry from 'full wages' as this account from an Aston (Birmingham) footplateman graphically illustrates: 'One of our drivers was on duty during a rather bad blitz when a land mine fell and exploded within 20 yards of his locomotive, inflicting great damage to the engine and serious injury to our brother, which caused him to lose one eye. Now this driver is a shed messenger. For his devotion to duty and harkening to the now-famous slogans "Carry On" and "Go To It," he has been reduced to shed labourer, deprived of all claim to the footplate; and also, as a generous gesture, deprived of the mean rate.

Now brothers does this reflect well on our Society? Do you think this is justice to a man who has served for 40 years handling trains during an air raid? No, brothers, I say certainly not! Why should we be degraded and cast asunder like dirt'? (C.E.Taylor Locomotive Journal; 1942, 115) It is worth remembering that the railways were guaranteed a profit for the duration of hostilities, which makes their own penny pinching attitudes even more unpalatable.

Ex-GCR Class 04 2-8-0, No.63601, a design used by the Railway Operating Division, during WW1, with a train of mineral empties for Rothley Brook sidings – GCR.

The 'owned' fighting and working to the death on behalf of the owners - or as the footplate historian, engine driver Norman McKillop, a.k.a Toram Beg, put it: 'It has been stated that the trade union movement took an unfair advantage of the war situation. I have not seen it asked whether the profit-making chaffering of world commerce, which lies at the bottom of all wars, considers it quite fair to ask the common man to sacrifice his life to secure these profits, and at the same time to deny him a reasonable share in them. (Mckillop, N. Lighted Flame a History of ASLEF p.109)

In December 1940 the Daily Mirror published an article, under the by-line "A Railway Official", accusing engine drivers of earning £15.00 per week. To earn this sum, on the rates of pay prevailing at the time, the drivers would have had to have been on duty for an unbelievable 148.5 hours. The Locomotive Journal provides a rather different account: 'I am aware of the lengthy hours of duty to which enginemen are being subjected, ... repeated approaches to the railway companies concerned [are being made] to get such hours of duty reduced very considerably. The reason these hours (up to 90) are being worked is because of the great number of men who have been released for service with the Forces and the lack of suitable recruits into the railway service to take their places.' (Locomotive Journal, 1941, 43/2)

The General Secretary asked the editors of the Daily Mirror that his statement be given the same prominence in the paper that the initial, "Railway Official", article had received: '...unfortunately, this courtesy was not extended to me in the same way. I hardly think it necessary to set out our opposition to such tactics, and am content to leave the above to speak for itself.' (Locomotive Journal, 1941, 42)

Ex-WD / Dutch / Swedish Railways 2-8-0, No.90733, banked by Ex-LMS Class 4F 0-6-0 No.43924, crossing Mytholmes viaduct with a goods train to Oxenhope – K&WVR.

This minor incident illustrates the way in which the Press not only manipulate the agenda but prevent a full discussion of the issues. When a man is forced by circumstances, not of his own making, to work many hours of overtime and as a result receives a larger than average pay-packet, is this a cause for approbation from the yellow press? There is also the issue of failing to give equal prominence to the General Secretary's reply, to the 'Railway Official'. This has a two-fold effect; the public are led to imagine that the engine drivers are profiteering from the war and that statements made by company officials are more credible and important than those of the Union's General Secretary, due to the prominence afforded to the former at the expense of the latter. In a modern context this is exactly what the Leveson Enquiry was all about. Press, media manipulation, and slurs aren't a new phenomenon in the everyday world of journalism.

Ex-LMS Class 3F 0-6-0T No.47406, blacking out Loughborough, as she departs with a local service to Rothley – GCR.

Another question you may well ask is why was there no story in the press about the shameless profiteering of the L.M.S. in overcharging footplatemen for the 'Iron Rations'? Undermining the 'Dunkirk' image of war-time Britain is only half the story. The treatment of the footplatemen by their employers, the press, and the Government is hardly conducive to improving morale, nor does it equate too well with the published images of footplate life. The representations of the lives of railway workers in the National Railway Museum, where the working class, White, Black, and Asian, as well as their respective historical and cultural inputs to the railways of Britain remain largely absent, is clearly in need of a dose of the 'realism' to be found in the pages of the Locomotive Journal.

At this junction we could be signalled into the loop to allow another of the 'Comforting Myths' to rush by. People can become quite angry if their particular comfort blanket is under siege but this shouldn't mean we don't lift the blanket. We may have brought railways to the world but it was those 'pesky Johnny foreigner types' who invented the bits which made them work more efficiently; the fire tube boiler is credited to the Frenchman Marc Seguin, the Injector to his fellow countryman Henri Giffard, Walschearts and his motion was Belgian, the superheater was introduced by a German engineer called, Schmidt, Belpaire's firebox, well that's Belgian too, and the Kylchap exhaust is a Finnish/French collaboration, then there's Caprotti valve gear that's Italian, and the A4's famous styling is really courtesy of Bugatti, another Italian – this sounds as though much British Locomotive engineering practice and design owes its existence to 'foreign engineering' rather than British. Some of these inventions, like Seguin's fire tube boiler, were essential to the success of the steam locomotive; one could probably say the same for Giffard's injectors: and Walschearts' motion, as well as Belpaire's firebox and Schmidt's superheater made very important contributions. All details we like to forget when the feuds begin over who was the 'greatest' locomotive designer or which was the 'best' locomotive class.

Ex-GWR 64xx Class 0-6-0PT, No.6430, alonside the river Dee, on the Llangollen Railway.

Comforting myths are the stock in trade of heritage railways and railway museums, especially the National Railway Museum. The NRM is like those old enamel signs, on stations with a curve in the platform, saying 'mind the gap' – only in the NRM's case behind the arc of history is the gap, well more of a chasm, between the real and the surreal. The NRM keep a long run of archive copies of the Railway Magazine, an influential magazine for railway enthusiasts, they do not have archive copies of the Locomotive Journal the monthly magazine of the engine driver's union, the Associated Society of Locomotive Engineers & Firemen. This is despite letters of complaint, newspaper articles, the fine words of a previous Keeper of the NRM, Mr Andrew Scott, and the passage of more than 10 years since the matter was first brought to light.

During this same period the NRM have managed to find millions of pounds to fritter on Flying Scotsman, whose repairs have now cost more than it did to build the A1 replica No. 60163 Tornado and if that wasn't enough they found even more money to ship expatriated A4 Class locomotives across the Atlantic to put on static display for the 75th anniversary of Mallard's 220yds at 126mph. This is a criminal waste of public money, without any historical justification and fulfilling just one purpose – to satisfy the boys and their toys mentality of the vast majority of putative 'railway enthusiasts'. What the NRM really celebrates are the middle-class fantasies of 'wannabe' engine drivers entirely at the expense of the working class, who built, ran, and maintained the railway and without whom there would not have been a railway let only a museum dedicated to them. The National Railway Museum is middle-brow, middle class, culture writ large and what an ugly spectacle it is – the only saving grace is that the engines look pretty.

Ex-GWR 2251 Class 0-6-0, No.3205, on Oldbury viaduct, Severn Valley Railway.

What tales are told and who tells them are really rather important. For example, the National Railway Museum uses its display of royal carriages to tell the public how Queen Victoria's train ride, which she 'enjoyed', helped to popularise the railway and the monarchy. It would have been just as easy to use these coaches to tell the public how Queen Victoria's government used the railways in the suppression of Chartism, or to contrast their opulence with the squalor that many of the people, involved both in Chartism and in the construction of the royal saloons, lived. Despite the overwhelming numbers of blue collar workers the railways employed, their role in the undertaking is virtually non-existent within the museum. Yet the head of the School of Railway History, Professor Colin Dival, in his inaugural lecture, in 1999, to the NRM & the Friends of the NRM said that; 'Museums and heritage attractions are some of the places where personal and collective memories can come together, where we make and reproduce the shared identities that help to define us all as social beings.' (Dival, type script, 1999, 4)

The only identities being shared and reproduced at the NRM are of white, middle class, males, there are no working class heroes as role models, no celebrations of the achievements of ordinary working men and women. No explanation of such important railway institutions as the enginemen's Mutual Improvement Class, even Wikipedia hasn't heard of the Mutual Improvement Class, or the enginemen's Mutual Assurance Fund. No explanation of the needs which led the railwaymen to create these institutions. Similarly there is no clear explanation of the creation of trade unions within the railway industry and no celebration of the men who formed or led these important institutions either. If we can celebrate Gresley, Bulleid, or Churchward then we can, most surely, celebrate Charles Perry and William Ullyott; their portraits should hang alongside those of Lord Stalbridge or George Leeman or any of the other 'great and good' – a phrase which usually covers a multitude of sinners, whose sins are, most likely, swept under the carpet.

Ex-LMS Class 5MT 4-6-0 No.44767, fitted with outside Stephenson's link motion, piloting Ex-LMS Class 5MT 4-6-0 No.44871 at the 'mound' near Oakworth – K&WVR.

I can hear the high horses being ridden, the how dares, and the, who does he think? – I've been there before. The philosopher Wittgenstein wrote; 'anything that can be said can be said clearly' a sentiment with which I wholeheartedly agree. Therefore, in the interest of clarity, the so called culture which creates and maintains establishments like the National Railway Museum is not only vacuous, but is clearly what the Philosopher Walter Benjamin had in mind when he wrote, 'they [the people] participate avidly in their own history while spectating it as someone else's history; they participate in political action and view it from a distance; they participate in their own destruction and enjoy the spectacle:'

A1 replica, 4-6-2, No. 60163 Tornado, safety valves open, crossing Montrose Basin en-route to Edingurgh with one of the series of GB rail tours.

Museums are held up, by a slew of social commentators, as institutions of cultural capital – it would, however, be infinitely more accurate to describe them as institutions of capital's culture. The NRM isn't a celebration of railwaymen and railways it's a celebration of corporate culture. It took the NRM more than 25 years, a string of complaints, and a damning newspaper article before they even got so far as putting driver Joe Duddington's name along with that of his fireman Tommy Bray, on the fastest steam locomotive of them all - Mallard. I have the letters from former Keeper, Andrew Scott, saying, basically, this was because of a lack of funds. What an insult both to Joe Duddington's memory and to my intelligence,  to say that, in 25 years they'd not had sufficient monies for a pot of paint and a display board. How glibly these people deal in terminological inexactitudes as they shuffle towards their OBE or handsome civil service pension, often both.

Culture, you've either got it or you haven't. Judging by what is on show in the NRM the working classes most definitely do not have a culture, or if they do it isn't on display in this institution of cultural capital. We don't give arts council grants to pigeon breeders; we don't give lottery funding to whippet racers. These may be exaggerated examples of working class stereotypes but the point is that there is, a working class culture, enjoyed by millions, which is completely ignored or marginalised within museum / arts council culture. I do not mean that there isn't a nod in the direction of putative 'common' culture, what I do mean is that there are no real celebrations of the achievements of that culture. A prime example of that attitude being the failure, over decades, to celebrate the role of Duddington and Bray in setting the world speed record for steam locomotive traction, as I discussed earlier.

Ex-BR Class 7P 4-6-2 No.70013 Oliver Cromwell, steams out of Loughborough Station – GCR. One of these engines, No.70047, remained un-named, throughout her existence.

The railway companies whose supposed triumphs are so lavishly exhibited within the NRM did not provide any formal training for their footplatemen. Ottley, the academic bibliography, (and bible), of railway publications, lists just one item under Mutual Improvement Class – a crib produced by a driver for the use of his fellow enginemen preparing for their driver's exams. During the heyday of steam driven railway travel there were more than 70,000 footplatemen – for most of them the Mutual Improvement Class provided the only 'training' they received – some of the railway companies even objected to the MIC, making it difficult for crews to hold them. At the depot where I began my career the MIC was held in the canteen after it ceased serving dinners, many others also used the canteen, out of hours, as their MIC room. The MIC classes were usually led by a driver or fitter but the way in which the classes were conducted encouraged participation by everyone – everyone was made to feel that they had a contribution to make – all knowledge was shared. This may not have been the case with all MIC's – especially as how they actually functioned on an individual level was very much determined by the staff at any one depot. However, the ethos of the MIC movement was very much one of shared knowledge and practical experience was as highly valued as book knowledge – the classes were held in a spirit of co-operation not competition, a very different learning situation to the normal master /pupil relationship in our schools and universities where competition is de rigeur. Having been both an attendee at MIC classes and a Grammar School and University student I can say that the pedagogic experience in the MIC classes was the more enjoyable one.

Ex-GWR 28xx Class 2-8-0, No.2807, heading for Oakworth, on the Keighley & Worth Valley Railway.

Heritage railways give out very clear signals in all their publicity material and there are, as you might expect, certain themes which occur over and over again; 'journey back in time', '25 years recreating history', 'an evening of pure nostalgia', are direct quotes from heritage railway promotional literature – a clear indication that what is on offer is a trip down memory lane. Just as the engineman learns the road by repeatedly travelling the route taking careful note of the salient features, passing loops, cross overs, positions, types, and numbers of signals, of under or over bridges, even stand out features in the landscape, so the heritage railway visitor remembers a route back to their past, through the smells of hot oil and sulphur given off by the engine, the enamelled advertisements on the station platform, semaphore signals, porters in serge uniforms, engine drivers in grease topped caps and blue cotton drills and the water colour paintings on the walls of the smoking or non-smoking compartments.

By way of a contrast to the 'evening of pure nostalgia', there's the 'charm' of the bed at the engineman's hostel still warm and the sheets all grubby, the pungent odour of the boilersmith's carbide lamp as he plies his trade in the confines of the firebox, or the 'true' romance of the footplate, 30 miles tender first, in a gale, in the wet, after being 'knocked up' at 2.00a.m. to go and do the job, or the adrenalin rush, and the rather troubling apprehension which follows it, generated by running over detonators in the fog – none of which appears in the brochures and isn't celebrated in the living tableaux the visitor experiences. However, these are daily and all too real experiences for generations of railway workers. It is perfectly understandable that people would not wish to be reminded of how unpleasant life could be especially if they were paying for the privilege. These are the wrong signals – they don't lead to halcyon days, no one wants to celebrate and re-live unpleasant memories. The problem is that all of this is every bit as much a part of what went on, on the railway, as all the 'nice' chocolate and cream coaches stuff.

Ex-L&Y 0-6-0, No.957, plods her way into Damems loop with a goods working from Keighley – K&WVR.

Distant signals, unlike home or starting signals are warning signals they give the driver a message about the next home signal. In the 'on' position, they show a yellow light which tells the driver to proceed with caution as the next home signal could/will be red. In the 'off' position they indicate that the road is 'clear' and the next home signal will be green – the practical effect of this is to allow trains to run faster if the signal is green. The 'distant signals' in the early railway landscape however, concerned very different circumstances; connecting services, the carriage of livestock and dangerous cargoes, even the width of the tracks was an issue not finally resolved until 1892, if indeed it ever was completely settled. Narrow gauge lines were being built, under Parliamentary attempts to stimulate parts of the rural economy, well into the 20th Century and the current Welshpool & Llanfair Railway is a part of one such line built in central Wales.

The attempts to deal with the novel and unforeseen issues created by the burgeoning network led to the formation of practices which ranged all the way from the pragmatic, via mediocre, through rank indifference on into borderline lunacy. Less obvious but no less important signals began to manifest themselves on many other levels too; from considerations on station architecture and locomotive design to what constituted corporate propriety and a reasonable working day/week for the company's employees. There is an aroma of constantly re-inventing the wheel hanging over the entire proceedings because of the free-for-all nature of Victorian capitalism. A plethora of competing schemes to build new lines created the platform for the departure of one of the earliest railway gravy trains and first on board were the legal profession whose job it was to prepare the Bills for Parliamentary approval. New railway technology brought new inventions and they meant more work for the legal eagles preparing and submitting patents.

Ex-GWR 45xx Class 2-6-2T, No.5542, with an Auto-train working from Loughborough to Rothley – GCR.

Competition didn't end with new lines, – all they did was breed the need for newer inventions, or create new possibilities for enterprise, such as the station bookstall, railway catering and the station buffet. On the engineering front there were competing designs in almost every aspect from the forms of valve gear used on the locomotives to the types of braking system, or lack thereof, on the rolling stock, and I've already mentioned the 'competing' forms of signalling. If this miasma of ideas and inventions had lead fairly rapidly to the general acceptance of 'best practice' one might have some sympathy for the supposed value of Victorian laissez faire capitalism.

They did no such thing, however. Arguments rage as fiercely today as they did 150 years ago as to what was or, for that matter, is 'best practice' – and amongst the Gricers this is nowhere more apparent than in the championing of one locomotive design / designer over another. Just as there are proverbs concerning the discussion of religion and politics in polite company so there should be for discussing locomotives/ locomotive designers in railway circles for nothing is guaranteed to start a feud quicker than one on the merits or demerits of a particular design/designer – well maybe one on liveries would be a very close run second.

Ex-LSWR M7 Class 0-4-4T, No. 53, with steam to spare, leaving Loughborough with a Leicester North service on the Great Central Railway.

By the time things got as far as selling tickets and the carrying of every conceivable type of cargo the vigorous competitive spirit of the age descended into near chaos. Important considerations on such matters as through ticketing and standard rates of charges for goods, and passengers alike was a distant aspect when the Nation was in thrall to railway mania and the lines began to proliferate way beyond those of the London & Birmingham, the Grand Junction, and the Liverpool and Manchester. The very mania for new routes and destinations spawned the institution whose role it was to try and make order out of the disorder. The Railway Clearing House came into being in 1842 and of the handful of Companies which formed the original committee one was none other than our old friend the Great North of England Railway or GNER for short. And round and round went the wheels on the bus, no on the train, well, no again, round and round go the wheels of history, one within another, on and on, creating a gigantic cosmic Spirograph which goes cart-wheeling off into the dim distance.

Ex-BR Class 5MT 4-6-0, No.73129, pilots Ex-LMS Class 5MT 4-6-0, No.45337, past Burrs, with a Bury – Rawtenstall service on the East lancashire Railway.

Clearing up the problems created by apportioning revenues to each company involved in moving goods or passengers from London to Liverpool, for instance, was mere child's play when compared to the shenanigans which took place at every point that the Broad Gauge met the Standard Gauge. Here the passengers and their luggage would be de-trained and re-trained, goods loaded and unloaded; it doesn't need a great deal of imagination to envisage the confusion, time wasted, luggage lost, goods damaged, tempers frayed. Again this was an issue which the competing companies refused to resolve until Parliament intervened – the broad gauge GWR opened in 1835 and it remained, defiantly, broad gauge until 1892. Despite losing the battle of the gauges the Great Way Round had the last laugh remaining more or less intact throughout the amalgamations, the grouping of 1923 and even into nationalisation as the Western Region. Inevitably one of the franchisees of the new train operating companies chose to incorporate 'Great' and 'Western' into its corporate image and choice of operating title. Hoping, no doubt, that a little bit of that chocolate and cream magic would rub off on their enterprise. Sadly, for them, they have become known as 'Worst Great Western'.

Ex-GWR City Class 4-4-0, No.3717 City of Truro, drifts out of Bewdley tunnel – SVR.

One flaw in the use of the railway's past to promote the railway's present is that in that past the railway was built not to the dictates of the accountancy department of a hedge fund, off-shore, in the Cayman Islands – which is why we still ride on a railway built 150 years ago. Yes there were scams and jerry-building but the overall ethos was one of building for permanence, quality materials and workmanship, a tendency towards 'over' engineering and, it has to be said, a desire to allay public fears and suspicions of what was a very new, untested, and on occasion, seriously, dangerous mode of travel. Railway travel and railway carriages today are undoubtedly safer than those of the Victorian era though I very much doubt that anyone today considers their modern coach more luxurious or comfortable than some of those on offer during Victoria's reign. Today it is unthinkable to present the present as anything other than 'the clean bright future'.  Today we live in a world increasingly connected to cyberspace, a world composed of growing levels of interaction with fleeting touch screen images, as one venerable Victorian rather presciently commented; 'everything that is solid melts into air', and so, today, it does.

One hundred and fifty years ago, solidity ruled – the railways wanted to show they were not some 'fly-by-night', 'here today gone tomorrow' industry – what better choice of words could there be to sum up this ambition than 'permanent way'. Laying the permanent way was just that – I guess you could say it does what it says, on the track if not on the tin. Constructing the P-way consumed vast quantities of stone, wood, steel, and iron, the infrastructure required equally vast quantities of, brick, glass, cement, plaster, and that's not counting the paint, the moquette, the horse hair stuffing, nor the mind-numbing numbers of workers whose labour, over many decades, created all of this stuff.

There's an element of self-perpetuation about the railways, more new lines meant more bricks for tunnels and bridges, more steel for engines and rail, more bricks and steel, more mines and more clay and all the bricks, the steel, and the clay had to be taken away by railways. More bricks, more steel, more bricks, more steel – clickety – click, clikety – cash. Dig more coal, mine more ores, build bigger engines – but not bigger men.

Ex-LSWR Class T9 4-4-0, No. 30120, just after departure from Bodmin Parkway, with a train for Bodmin General and Boscarne Junction, on the Bodmin & Wenford Railway.

Further and faster, quicker and longer, more bricks, more rails, set up a workshop, build a new town, dig more coal, open new pits, need more lines – my head's beginning to revolve. The railway enterprise not only created expansion in the mining, iron, steel, and brick industry it spawned entirely new occupations, signal and telegraph engineers, platelayers, timetablers, booking office clerks, wheel-tappers and their side-kicks the shunters, are just the merest fraction of the new jobs on the market and existing companies, making everything from the lenses for the signal lamps to the weavers who made the cloth for the upholstery in the coaches, saw a huge expansion of their order books.

The growth in manufacturing simply to supply the multifarious needs of the railway industry was a booming business – and dynamite was high on the list. Unfortunately, explosives weren't the only things exploding – steam boilers could and did go with a bang. Sometimes the boiler's burst because of faulty manufacture, but on other occasions the cause was human intervention or simply inattention.

Ex-LMS Class 5MT 4-6-0, No.44871, leaving Oakworth with a train for Oxenhope – K&WVR.

There's an apocryphal story about Richard Trevithick's first engine exploding, after the boiler ran dry, whilst Trevithick and crew whet their whistles in a nearby Inn. There's also the well documented case from Charles Brandling's colliery railway, in Leeds. In 1818 'engine-man' George Hutchinson was killed when the boiler of his engine 'Salamanca' exploded. The local Leeds paper the Leeds Mercury had this to say, 'James Hewitt, the first witness, stated that: ... he worked the engine called the Lord Wellington: the deceased, George Hutchinson, had care of the engine which exploded, called Salamanca. He stated that all the Engine-men had directions from Mr.Blenkinsop, never to have the steam at a higher pressure than fifty-five pounds the square inch, but that the deceased had several times had the steam raised to a much higher pressure.' (Leeds Mercury 07/03/1818 from a History of the Middleton Railway Leeds 8th ed. p29) Several years earlier, in 1813, George Butler, another of the line's drivers, had lost his right hand in the running gear after falling from the footplate whilst firing the engine.

These incidents clearly indicate the dangers which could befall the unwary. 'Weighting' the safety valves might have been warned against but, in real life, people would take chances to 'get the job done'. We can only imagine the temperamental nature of the fledgling technology but it doesn't require a great leap to imagine that gaining a few extra pounds of steam pressure might be a big help in getting the train moving and keeping it going. Driver Hutchinson, it seems, was a little more blasé about this activity than some of the other crew at Brandling's Colliery. Weighting the safety valves was a not uncommon feature on many an early locomotive and driver Hutchinson was certainly not alone in carrying on this dubious practice.

(Increased boiler pressure means that an engine might; pull more weight, or simply go further for longer. The early locomotives were probably not the best of steamers, and knowledge of how to raise steam on them would have been very much trial and error – simply having more steam meant you went further before having to stop for a blow-up. In 1818, when Brandling's engine exploded, steam locomotives were in a very primitive state of development, and someone like the hapless driver would have little or no idea of the consequences which might arise from his foolhardy actions.)

Manning Wardle 0-6-0ST, Sir Berkeley, pilots Bagnall 0-4-0ST Matthew Murray, under the M1 motorway, on the remanants of Brandlings colliery railway – the present day Middleton Railway.

Boiler explosions on steam locomotives, in factories, and in mines led directly to the creation of one of the more important 'societies' in the 19th century The Manchester Society for the Prevention of Boiler Explosions – a lineage which comes right through to today's boiler inspector and the thorough and detailed examinations they make of locomotive fireboxes and boilers, before passing them fit for steaming. It wasn't altruism which brought about the Manchester Society but economics – when boilers exploded they wrecked expensive capital equipment, reduced or halted production and ruined existing stock. Workers were the least expensive part of the equation and there was no shortage of supply. Orphanages, very often church orphanages, provided a steady supply of cheap child labour to the mills, mines, and factories.

The new jobs and businesses created by the growing industrialisation needed a new kind of workforce, knowing which way up to plant a potato wasn't going to help you read a set of instructions or write out a weigh bill. To ensure that there were sufficient numerate and literate workers to staff the new undertakings the Government passed the 1844 Education Act, providing for basic schooling, in reading, writing, and arithmetic for many, if not all, children. Railway companies were amongst the first to reap the benefits of the creation of Mechanics Institutes, the first one opened in Edinburgh in 1821 and they rapidly spread across Britain. The first one in England opened in Liverpool in 1824 and at their height there were more than 700 across the country. Mechanics Institutes provided for the 'training of working men' as civil and mechanical engineers, draughtsmen, and, in due course, electrical engineers. Some of these Mechanics Institutes became such large and important institutions that they formed the building blocks of a goodly number of modern day Universities. The Mechanics Institutes in places like Crewe, Swindon, and Derby were practically off shoots of, respectively, the London North Western, the Great Western and the Midland railways – with railway managers and appointees holding places on the governing bodies.

Ex-BR Britannia Class 4-6-2, No.70013 Oliver Cromwell, near Quorn & Woodhouse – GCR.

Creating an educated workforce was as essential to the success of the industrial revolution, as the availability of the raw materials – an educated workforce is a kind of raw material. The railway provided an impetus to the spread of new ideas and new knowledge in two distinct ways. On the simple and direct level they allowed people to move around the country more easily, a jargon term might read something along the lines of – they facilitated the spread of human discourse by creating new milieu in which it could take place. The railways provided the mechanical means for ideas to spread at the face to face level far easier and faster than previously, they also speeded up the postal services, thus speeding up the process of indirect communication too. On the technological level they had another effect. Today we live in a world where we can communicate globally, instantly, and at very minimal cost – when the railway age dawned communications which, previously, had taken days, or weeks in many cases, could be made in hours. As the railway telegraph system spread, communications became almost instant by comparison – who can forget all those 'telegram boys' on their bicycles or BSA Bantam motor cycles. Such was the size and complexity of the railway telephone and telegraph system that it was second only to the GPO during the steam railway era.

Ex-LMS Class 2 2-6-2MTT No.41241, banked by Ex-BRClass 4MTT 2-6-4, No.80002, with a goods working to Damems loop – K&WVR.

Very high levels of information, along with ease of access to it, on practically every topic from the proximity of Asteroids, to a treatment for haemorrhoids, or even the whereabouts of the nearest Zoo are so embedded in all aspects of life today, that we take them entirely for granted but, when the railway age began; gathering, disseminating, and making practical use of the information that was available was in an even less advanced state than the crude mechanical inventions which powered the early industrial revolution. However, the railways were, unquestionably, an exponential growth factor in the spread of ideas, information and culture. The odd thing about heritage railways is that whilst they are very much a part of culture their relationship to it is almost the polar opposite of the railway's original place in culture. Heritage railways are, by definition, backward looking; their own publicity material proclaims that travelling back in time is the reason to visit them.

Ex-GWR Manor Class 4-6-0, No.7822 Foxcote Manor chugs into Glyndyfrdwy station, as Ex-BR Class 4MTT 2-6-4, No.80072 awaits the road - Llangollen Railway.

Railway builders, promoters, and shareholders in the 1830s, 40s, 50s, etc., weren't looking back when the railway age commenced, they all had their eyes firmly on the future – a prosperous, happy, future, with the railways conquering all before them. They were inventing 'this is how it's done' on a daily basis – they were 'going places' literally as well as figuratively. This is an entirely different world view from the one which emphasises past achievements, former glories, arcane knowledge and the supposed safety of the tried and tested.

However, there's a much more fundamental problem, (strange how frequently fundamental ends up not being a lot of fun and often seriously mental), when it comes to dealing with the historical version of 'time flies by when you're the driver of a train'. In this view time is experienced as 'tradition' – the Great Western Railway's historic use of brass and copper on their locomotives, or the London North Eastern Railway's association with teak coaches, for example. This view applies to traditional social values just as much as it does to locomotives and rolling stock - traditional values assume a status they never enjoyed until a period of 'time had elapsed'. Our experiences of time differ wildly which, given its manmade nature, is not unsurprising, experiencing time as 'tradition' is the default mode for the heritage railways and their visitors. The philosopher Walter Benjamin described time experienced as tradition as 'a place of mourning'; that is as a sadness, a longing for what has passed and gone. Later he modified his view to incorporate the idea that time experienced as tradition was 'political'

('The site of tradition is always one of ruination, a place of mourning. Those who gathered there did not do so in order to decide who they were … but in order to mourn.' 'The place where past, present and future are gathered in tradition is no longer one of mourning, but one of politics.' Caygill, H. Benjamin, Heidegger and the Destruction of Tradition.)

Ex-BR Class 4MTT 2-6-4, No.80105, departs from Kinneil Halt, with a mixed train for Birkhill, on the Bo'ness & Kinneil Railway.

Benjamin's political opposite and near contemporary, Martin Heidegger, held a surprisingly similar view and he was quite explicit when it came to material objects from the past:  'The act of 'handing over' destroys the object it surrenders; it is in no sense a 'medium', let alone a neutral medium for the transmission of the past to the present.' (Caygill,H. Benjamin, Heidegger and the Destruction of Tradition.)

I'm well aware that these philosophical views do not detract one iota from the enjoyment and pleasure to be gained from visiting and journeying on a heritage railway but they do have very serious implications for the claims that heritage railways play some kind of historical /educational role. Heritage railways are, perhaps, best summed up by the neologism 'infotainment'; that is entertainment which, as a by-product, imparts some level of information along with the entertainment. This is not a criticism, merely a statement about the limitations of the heritage railways abilities to create meaningful insights into the nature of railways, railwaymen, and railway work, as historical entities. When we come to questions of funding, or of politics, then these philosophical views should become more of an issue than they appear to have been. That they have not played a more important role is a matter of politics, not politics on the grand global level, nor even on a party political one, but at the level of expediency.

Ex-LNER B1 Class 4-6-0 No.1306 Mayflower leaves Berwyn station, on the Llangollen Railway, bearing the 'Mayflower' head board – a Paddington – Plymouth service.

Heritage railways have undoubtedly helped to create jobs, boost tourism, and they train apprentices in once common skills and as such they are entitled to consider themselves a benefit to the economy and the country. I have, over the years, met Dutch, German, French, Italian, and American railway enthusiasts at events and galas on railways all around the country - many of them regular visitors to these events. I know from the railways own visitor's books that people come from all corners of the globe to enjoy what has been saved, restored and operated.

Some lines are a valued part of the local transport system and offer discounted travel to local residents; at one time, the Romney Hythe and Dymchurch Railway, a narrow gauge line across the Romney marshes, held the railway equivalent of the 'school bus contract' taking local youngsters to school each day. I must add however, that the RH&DR, isn't, strictly speaking, a heritage railway. In the Second World War the RH&DR was part of the nation's front-line defences and there was even a special 'armoured train' complete with anti-tank gun. In Yorkshire, the Keighley & Worth Valley Railway offer local residents a discount travel concession and both the

North Yorkshire Moors Railway and the Swanage Railway have been involved with trying to implement park and ride schemes in the North Yorkshire Moors National Park in the NYMR's case and onto the Isle of Purbeck in the Swanage case. It is the heritage railway's ability to help in the process of economic regeneration which has led to its support across the political spectrum, with the possible exception of the Green Party whose objection isn't economic but environmental.

Ex-LMS Class 5MT 4-6-0, No.45231 Sherwood Forester, at Dalgety Bay, with one of the Scottish Railway Preservation Society's 'Fife Circle' rail tours.

Working in partnership with local councillors, County councillors and members of Parliament the heritage railways have created funding networks way beyond holding raffles and selling railwayana and bric-a-brac to raise money. Help with infrastructure projects, bridge and access maintenance, (when the M1 motorway entered Leeds the constructors were forced to put a bridge over the Middleton Railway's line just outside the Moor Road terminus), are all part and parcel of the co-operation between the heritage railway industry and all forms of government. In North Wales an entire narrow gauge railway, abandoned in the 1930s, which ran between Caernarvon and Porthmadog has, for all practical purposes, been entirely rebuilt. If this wasn't enough the line, which tackles some serious gradients along its route, is powered, in part, by Garrett type steam locomotives repatriated from South Africa. While significant sums of money were generated by private means local, National, and European government money alongside Heritage Lottery funding has helped to bring this truly ambitious project to completion.

Ex-SAR NGG Class 16 2-6-2+2-6-2, No. 87, in workshop 'photo' grey livery, runs round at Beddgellert Station, on the Welsh Highland Railway.

Funding and the state of the infrastructure were not the only obstacles in re-opening this route; just as with so many things in the modern as well as the Victorian world, there were objectors. The original Welsh Highland line was not without its objectors and I do believe there was some sort of double-dealing involving the North Wales Power & Light Co. in actually getting parliamentary approval for the original line. There was little new in this as any student of railway politics and rivalries will attest but, it does serves as a reminder of just how much 'in the balance' some railways were. The really remarkable thing about this particular line is despite its closure in 1938 and a bitter legal battle between two groups of preservationists, as to which one should/ would / could rebuild and run it, a scene more reminiscent, perhaps, of the battle between Hudson and the Stockton & Darlington Board in the 1840s, it is up and running. Despite, who knows, maybe even because of all the difficulties it did rise from the dead to provide one of the most scenic railway journeys in the whole of Britain with views of Snowdon and the route through the Aberglaslyn Pass amongst the highlights.

We are, now, a very long way from those 'make it up as you went along' days of the railway's and preservation's early history, and even further from those days on the platform ends. Now the latest fashion is to slavishly follow HSE directives, prosecute trespass, and insist that all who do go trackside have a PTS course and matching certificate. What a contrast with how it was, when shed bashing meant tresspassing and straying trackside didn't even merit a hi-vis vest. Today the 'railway children' are mature adults being treated like children – how have we allowed that to happen?

Robert Stephenson 0-6-0T, No.3 Twizell, with a Santa service crossing Causey Arch car park bridge on the Tanfield Railway

Speaking for myself; the very idea that I could be taught, by 'amateur' railwaymen, how to conduct myself on the lineside of some heritage railway after spending years of my life running real trains, and over some of the most heavily used routes in the country, is almost laughable. My objection is that from what I've witnessed, over more than 30 years of visits to heritage lines, the shambolic amateurism, the lack of basic train handling skills, and, on occassions dangerous and stupid practices – I have forgotten more than most preservation footplate crews know. This isn't to be arrogant, or big-headed, it is simply a statement of fact. Spending more than 7 years working, for 50 weeks a year, and anything from 50 to 70 hours a week, on average, with every conceivable category of train, and over every type of railway, your own personal safety and that of the travelling public become a part of your life in a way that chugging up and down at 20 or even 25mph over 10 or 20 miles of track, for a few weekends each year, just doesn't.

The continued growth of the risk averse, risk managed, lifestyle is one of the least pleasant aspects of modern life. In fact the assumption that because some folk are incapable of functioning in a civilised and responsible manner that we are all in need of nannying is, probably, the most annoying of all current assumptions about daily life and activity. All of which brings me to the conclusion of this railway ramble. We've travelled from those carefree days of childhood to a controlled and controlling adulthood, we no longer risk being chased off shed by the running shed foreman, or climb a wall behind the 'shed' to bunk in the back way – not even railway preservation can bring that back.

'That's All Folks'

Printed in Great Britain
by Amazon